EUROPE
OCÉAN GLACIAL
OCÉAN ATLANTIQUE
ILES BRITANNIQUES
MER DU NORD
Cercle Polaire Arctique
I. de Jean Mayen
Is. Faroer
LA MANCHE
G. de Gascogne
MER MÉDITERRANÉE
MER IONIENNE
MER ADRIATIQUE
MER BALTIQUE
G. DE BOTHNIE
DANEMARK
FRANCE
SUISSE
ESPAGNE
PORTUGAL
AFRIQUE
Paris
Lisbonne
Madrid
Londres
Amsterdam
Berlin
Stockholm
Copenhague
Vienne
Naples
Rome
Alger
Barcelone
Gibraltar

PLM

THE VINCENT VAN GOGH ATLAS

Nienke Denekamp
& René van Blerk
With illustrations by Geert Gratama

Translation Laura Watkinson

RUBINSTEIN
VAN GOGH MUSEUM

CONTENTS

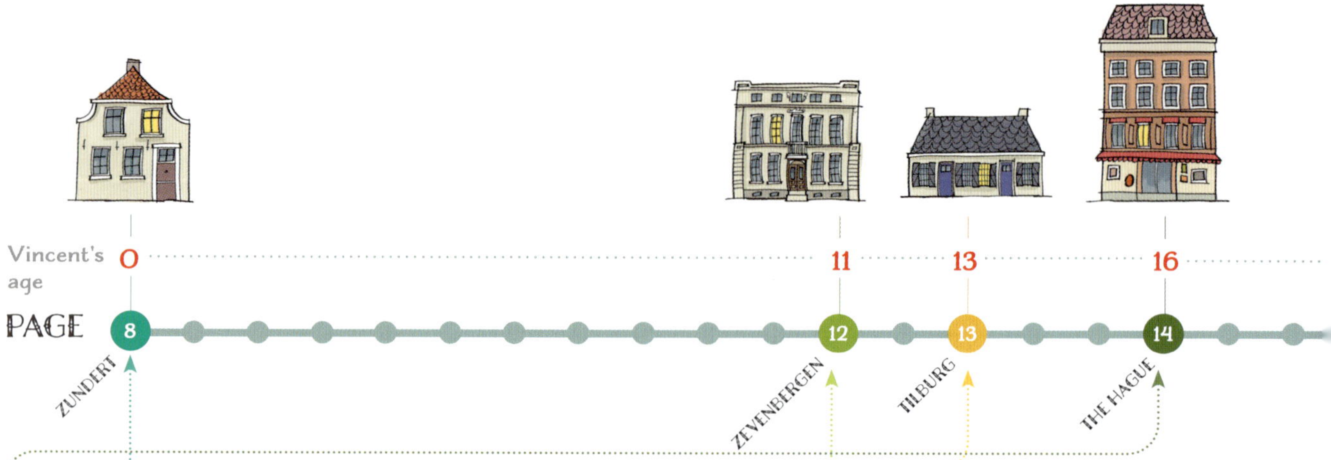

5 Introduction

8 Zundert 1853–1864

12 Zevenbergen 1864–1866

13 Tilburg 1866–1868

14 The Hague 1869–1873

25 London 1873–1875

33 Paris 1874–1876

35 England 1876

37 Dordrecht 1877

41 Amsterdam 1877–1878

49 The Borinage (Belgium) 1878–1880

54 Brussels 1880–1881

57 Etten 1881

THE VINCENT van GOGH ATLAS

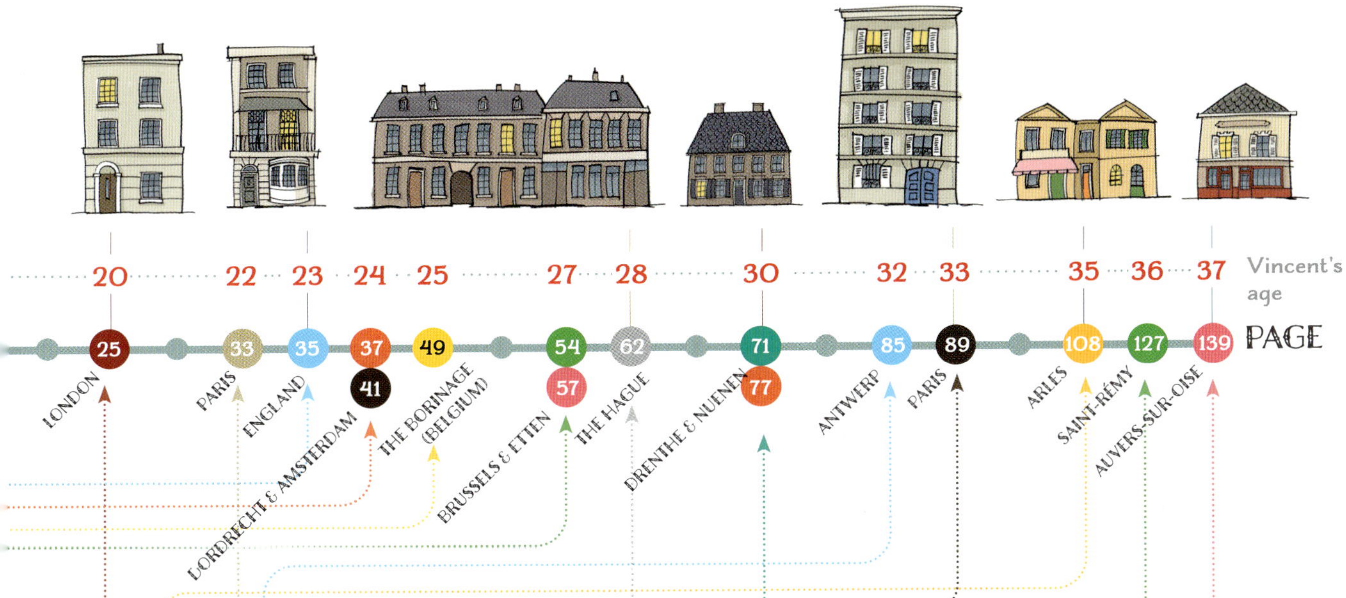

62 The Hague 1881–1883
71 Drenthe 1883
77 Nuenen 1883–1885
85 Antwerp 1885–1886
89 Paris 1886–1888
108 Arles 1888–1889
127 Saint-Rémy 1889–1890
139 Auvers-sur-Oise 1890
148 After Vincent's death

England
London
North Sea
Amsterdam
Netherlands
Zundert
Belgium
Auvers-sur-Oise
Paris
France
LAND
WATER
RAILWAY LINE
PLACES WHERE VINCENT LIVED
(CITY / VILLAGE)

INTRODUCTION

VINCENT VAN GOGH is a world-famous artist. You've probably seen a painting by him somewhere before. *Sunflowers*, for example, or *The Starry Night*. If you ask people what they know about him, nearly everyone says, 'His ear!' or 'That poor artist! No one understood him!'

But not many people know Vincent's whole story. That's what we're going to tell you here. This book will take you with Vincent from Z to A: from Zundert in the southern Netherlands (where he was born) to Auvers-sur-Oise in France (where he died). We'll stop off at lots of different places in the Netherlands, England, Belgium and France. Was Vincent's end also the end of his story? Fortunately not! For many people, Vincent still lives on today – in his drawings and paintings.

All his life, Vincent was curious about things. He liked to go for long walks in the countryside, and through towns and villages that he didn't know yet. But there always came a time when he wanted to leave – to go to another village, another town, another country. Vincent travelled thousands of kilometres. On foot. In carriages, or on boats. But especially on steam trains! They were very modern at the time. When Vincent was born (in 1853), there weren't many railway lines in Europe. But by the time he was an adult, he was able to travel almost anywhere by train. At high speed! Although... trains didn't actually go any faster than fifty kilometres an hour.

Steam trains transported people, and also post. Letters were sometimes delivered up to four times a day, at home and abroad. That was handy because people didn't have telephones or the internet back then. But when you're far away from your family and friends, you obviously want to let them know how you're doing. So did Vincent. His younger brother Theo, in particular, received post from Vincent every week. Vincent sent him letters and also the drawings and paintings that he made. And Theo kept everything: every letter, every painting, every sketch and scribble. As a result, we now have around 850 of Vincent's paintings, 1,300 drawings and more than 800 letters. They all tell a piece of Vincent's story.

Vincent liked reading books more than playing with the other children in the school playground, and he loved nature. He spent hours wandering on the heath and through the meadows, woods and marshes around Zundert.

ZUNDERT

1853–1864

The birthplace

This picture shows **the house where Vincent was born**, in the middle of the village of Zundert, in the south of the Netherlands. That house no longer exists. It was demolished more than a hundred years ago. No one knew at the time that it was the house where the world's most famous artist had been born. There is only one photograph with the house in it. This one. It happened by chance when the photographer wanted to take a picture of the man in the carriage, who was celebrating his hundredth birthday.

Vincent's parents were very respectable. They had household staff: a maid, two cooks and a gardener. The Van Gogh family went for a walk around the village every day – **Vincent's mother** in her hoop skirt, and **his father** in a top hat. The children followed behind, all dressed in nice clothes. Vincent was the eldest child. He had three sisters and two brothers. He slept in an attic room with his brother Theo, both in the same bed.

MOTHER

FATHER

The Van Gogh family

Vincent's father was a church minister by profession. He led the services on Sundays and told people from the village about God and the Bible. Minister Van Gogh was very popular. When someone in the village was ill, he went to visit them. Sometimes he also paid for groceries for poor people. Everyone knew him, as he used to ride through the village in a yellow horse-drawn carriage.

Vincent's mother was always busy with jobs in and around the house. She taught her children to draw and make things and gave them exciting books to read. Devices like smartphones, tablets and television hadn't been invented yet. There was plenty of time in the evening to read books to each other, to play board games or to write long letters.

Mrs Van Gogh told her children all about plants and animals. That was nice for Vincent, who loved nature. He wandered for hours across the heathland and through the meadows, the woods and the marshes around Zundert, or he went down to the stream to catch beetles. Then he would pin them in white cardboard boxes and write their names beside them. He knew all their names by heart. Like his brothers and sisters, he was very fond of the garden behind the house. It had brightly coloured flowers and a vegetable garden with bushes full of **raspberries** and currants.

Sadly, the Van Goghs' first child was stillborn. He was also called Vincent. His famous brother was born a year later, on exactly the same date: 30 March.

VINCENT

ANNA

THEO

LIES

WILLEMIEN

COR

The town hall in Zundert.

Vincent lived directly opposite the primary school.

The school

The primary school was opposite the **Van Goghs' house**. That was where Vincent and his brothers and sisters learned to read, write and do sums. Much later, after Vincent had become famous, his schoolmates told people that he had just been an ordinary boy – not the kind of person you thought would be a famous painter one day. He would rather read a book than play with other children in the playground. He was often quiet. Hardly anyone remembered Vincent being good at drawing. Sadly, none of the drawings he did as a child has survived.

Here you can see **the school** and here is the Van Gogh family's **house**.

ZEVENBERGEN AND

1864–1866

Boarding school and host family

When Vincent was eleven, he went to a school for respectable 'young gentlemen and young ladies' in Zevenbergen. That was twenty-five kilometres away: half an hour in a car these days, but more than two hours in his father's carriage. It was a boarding school, where children also had to live. They only went home during the school holidays. Vincent's parents took him to the school. When they said goodbye and drove away down the street, Vincent felt terribly lonely. He was very homesick in Zevenbergen. He said later that he had learned nothing there.

It is hard to see him, but this is Vincent, with a cap on his knees. The schoolteachers all wore hats.

TILBURG
1866–1868

After that, he went on to secondary school in Tilburg. During the week, he stayed with a 'host family' who lived close to the school. Vincent's parents paid them to look after him. Luckily, he was allowed to go home at the weekends. That was possible because there was a railway line between Tilburg and Breda. Vincent had to walk for another three hours when he got to Breda, but he didn't mind the walk. Not much is known about this time in Vincent's life. We know he was one of the best students in his class and that he got good grades when he moved up into the next year. But then he suddenly left the school before the May holiday. Did he get into a fight? Was he suffering from homesickness again? We don't know. Whatever happened, Vincent went back home. Once again, he had lots of time to spend all day roaming through the countryside around Zundert.

Train ticket from Rosendaal to Tilburg.

Vincent travelled from Breda to Tilburg by steam train.

The school in Tilburg.

The train

We think that it's perfectly normal these days to get into a car and drive somewhere. But when Vincent was a boy, that wasn't the case. Cars didn't exist yet. Only rich people could afford a carriage. There was a new mode of transport that had recently been invented, though: the steam train. They were spectacular machines that made an incredible amount of noise and puffed out big clouds of steam. Railway lines were being constructed all over the world, more and more of them every year. When Vincent was at school, there were enough railway lines to go around the globe three times. Twenty years later, it was fifteen times.

The railway line that Vincent travelled along to school, from Breda to Tilburg, had been in operation for only three years. It really was a very new way to travel. However, the steam train didn't go very quickly. Nowadays it takes twelve minutes to go by train from Breda to Tilburg. In Vincent's day, it was half an hour. It didn't go any faster than fifty kilometres an hour. However, that was still a lot faster than his father's carriage.

THE HAGUE
1869–1873

This is what Uncle Cent's art shop looked like on the inside.

At work

Vincent didn't enjoy his time at school, but he obviously couldn't spend all day wandering around the countryside. So, his parents told him he needed to get a job. When he was sixteen, they arranged a job for him in the fashionable city of The Hague. Vincent became an assistant at a gallery, a shop that sold art. The walls were filled from top to bottom with new works of art by famous artists. People would often pause outside to look at the paintings in the display windows. The gallery belonged to an uncle of Vincent's, who was also called Vincent. His nephews and nieces called him Uncle Cent, perhaps because he had made a lot of cents by selling art and had become very wealthy.

Uncle Cent

Not everyone was able to fill their house with paintings. Art was expensive. But **Uncle Cent**'s gallery also sold pictures of paintings: prints. They were a lot cheaper. The painting was copied onto a metal plate with a needle. You could then use the plate and ink to make lots of prints on paper. It was also possible to make copies by taking a photograph of a painting. That might sound obvious to us, but it wasn't obvious at the time. Photography was still very new back then. Vincent had his own collection of prints. He pinned them to the walls of his room.

The display window at Goupil in The Hague.

Uncle Cent worked with the owners of other galleries in **Paris, Brussels, Berlin, London and New York**. They had agreed that all their businesses should be called 'Goupil & Cie', a fancy French name, which was good for advertising. Uncle Cent was hardly ever at the gallery in The Hague because he spent a lot of time travelling. He lived with Aunt Cornelia in a huge house in Breda, and they also had a home in Paris.

When he was working in The Hague, Vincent had more to do with Hermanus Tersteeg, who was the boss when Uncle Cent was not around. Mr Tersteeg taught Vincent a lot about painting and gave him jobs to do every day. Sometimes he had to pack paintings in crates and take them to the post office. At other times he helped with the display windows. Vincent was proud of his job. He got along well with his boss, who lived above the gallery with his wife and three-year-old daughter Betsy. Whenever Betsy saw Vincent, she smiled.

AGENTUUR

Uncle Cent's shop.

Goupil's printing shop in Paris.

These are examples of prints from the Goupil printworks.

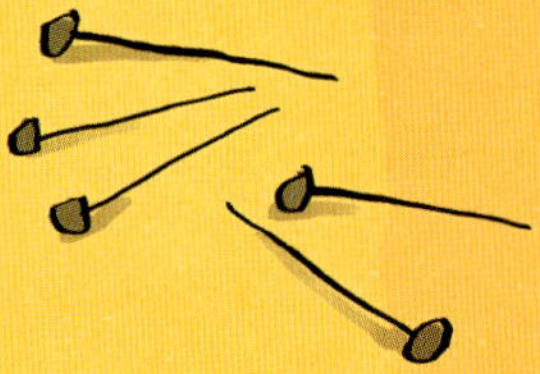

Vincent collected prints of his favourite paintings. He bought them for himself and sometimes gave them as gifts to Theo or his father as well. In all the rooms where he lived, he only felt at home when he could pin his prints to the walls. His landlords were not always happy about that. When Vincent moved out, he left behind a wall full of holes.

Walks

Vincent also stayed with a family in The Hague. They were nice people. They didn't even mind Theo coming to stay for a few days. **Vincent**, who was now nineteen, was able to show his fifteen-year-old brother around the city. They visited the Mauritshuis, a museum, where he told Theo about the famous paintings on the walls. They walked in the rain along the beach at Scheveningen and through the meadows around The Hague, stopping at a windmill for a glass of milk. Vincent was happy that Theo was there. They agreed that they would be friends forever. When Theo returned home, he wrote a letter to his big brother. Vincent wrote back to him right away. From then on, they continued writing to each other, all their lives. Theo kept everything, so all his letters from Vincent, more than 650 of them, have survived. Everyone can read them online. Sadly, we have only 41 of Theo's letters to Vincent. Once Vincent had read a letter, he usually threw it into the stove.

Vincent at the age of nineteen. The photograph was a gift for his father's 51st birthday.

Sadly, no pictures that Vincent drew as a child have survived. This is one of the oldest ones we know, from when he was around twenty years old. It is the lake at the Binnenhof in The Hague, the meeting place of the Dutch parliament. Vincent walked past here every day, on his way to work.

Leaving The Hague

Later, Theo went to work at Goupil as well, but in Brussels. They were very pleased with him. Things were not going as well for Vincent, though. After four years, he was transferred to Goupil in London. Mr Tersteeg was not so happy with him anymore. Vincent knew a lot about art, so that was not the problem, but he was far too opinionated and not nice enough to the customers. He argued with them if he thought they'd chosen the wrong painting. A lot of art was stored at the Goupil warehouse in London, so there was plenty of work to do, but customers didn't come to visit. Mr Tersteeg thought it might be a better place for Vincent. But Vincent himself didn't want to go to London at all. He would much rather have stayed with his friends in The Hague.

Vincent didn't forget his friends after he left the city. He sometimes filled **notebooks with funny drawings of animals**, like a dog smoking a pipe and a cat drinking tea, for the young Betsy Tersteeg. These notebooks were delivered by Theo, who had taken Vincent's place at the gallery in The Hague.

Vincent bought a top hat, as that was the fashion in London. Now he felt like a true citizen of the world.

In Dieppe, the steam train stopped next to the boat to England.

LONDON

1873–1875

An omnibus in London. These 'buses' had no engines: like a carriage, they were pulled by horses.

Big cities

Vincent didn't have to travel alone. Uncle Cent and Aunt Cornelia took him to London. They journeyed by train via Paris, a city where Vincent had never been before. He slept and dined at his aunt and uncle's elegant apartment. A few days later, they left for London. In Vincent's day, London was the biggest city in the world and the only place where you could travel by underground train. The streets were packed with people pushing handcarts and riding in carriages, all wanting to get somewhere. Everything in London was different from what Vincent had known in the Netherlands. When he didn't have to work, he wandered through the city for hours, just looking around. Sometimes he stopped for a moment to make a drawing to send home in a letter.

Via Paris to London

These days you can travel by train from Paris to London in less than two and a half hours. It took Vincent and his aunt and uncle more than fourteen hours. They had to travel about seven hours first, by train from The Hague to the port of Dieppe. The train used to stop right at the dock for the steamer that sailed to Newhaven in England once a day. In the summer, it was a pleasant boat journey of five hours but in the winter it took longer. In bad weather, the travellers got shaken around. Sometimes people were seasick. When you arrived in England, there was a train waiting for the boat, which took travellers to London in two hours.

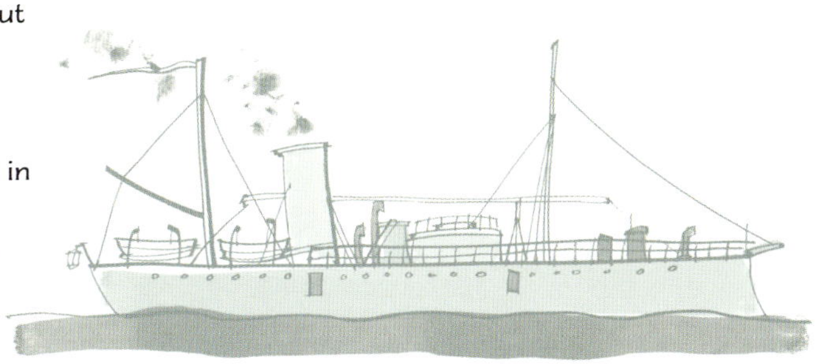

Vincent thought Rotten Row in Hyde Park was one of the most beautiful places in the city. It was a long and wide avenue, where London's wealthiest ladies and gentlemen went up and down on horses and in carriages. Seeing and being seen – that was what it was all about. Vincent bought a top hat, as that was the fashion. He had been to Paris, lived in London and now he felt like a true citizen of the world.

Parrots and a piano

Vincent lived in various boarding houses in London. The first one was so far away that he had to take a steamboat along the River Thames every day to go to work. Vincent wrote to Theo that there were also two parrots living at the boarding house and three Germans, who played the piano and sang songs. He told him which paintings he had seen in the museums and galleries in London, and he sent him a list of his favourite painters, sixty-two in total. Vincent had some good advice for his sixteen-year-old brother, too. It was important to walk a lot, he wrote. If you spent time looking at beautiful things in nature, you became better and better at understanding art. He also thought Theo should start smoking a pipe, as he did himself. People in Vincent's day didn't know how unhealthy it is to smoke.

The marriage proposal

It became too expensive for Vincent to travel to work by steamboat every day, so he rented a room closer to his job. **The house** belonged to a schoolteacher and her daughter, and he got along well with them. Vincent wrote enthusiastic letters about the two ladies to his family in the Netherlands. But after a while his letters became less happy. His parents thought he was thin and quiet when he returned to the Netherlands for a holiday. He had apparently asked the schoolteacher's daughter to marry him, but she had said no, because she was already engaged to someone else. His family were worried. When Vincent was transferred to Paris, his mother was relieved. She thought it would do him good.

The post

In Vincent's time, there were a lot of changes in the postal system. That was because of the railway lines that were being built. Trains full of letters and parcels could travel faster and faster to more and more places. Postmen sometimes called four times a day to deliver a letter, a card or a parcel. The post was obviously not as fast as calling someone by phone, but hardly anyone could do that at the time. Although the telephone had been invented, it was years before people had one at home. So, giving someone a quick call was not an option. However, it was possible to send a card in the morning from The Hague to Amsterdam to say that you wouldn't be able to make it to dinner that evening – and the card would arrive in time.

Vincent always stayed in touch with his family by post, no matter where he lived. And he wasn't the only Van Gogh to be so far from home at a young age. One of his sisters attended boarding school in Friesland, in the north of the Netherlands, and two of them went to work in England. Theo was first in Brussels, then in The Hague, and later in Paris. Vincent's youngest brother Cor even went to live in South Africa. The Van Gogh children wrote long letters to tell the rest of the family what they were doing. Or what the place where they were living was like. They sent one another presents, such as books, photographs, chocolate, clothes and money, but also dried flowers or a piece of seaweed from the beach. Later, when Vincent was an artist, Theo even sent him ten stamps one time. Vincent was delighted – it meant he could write and send even more letters.

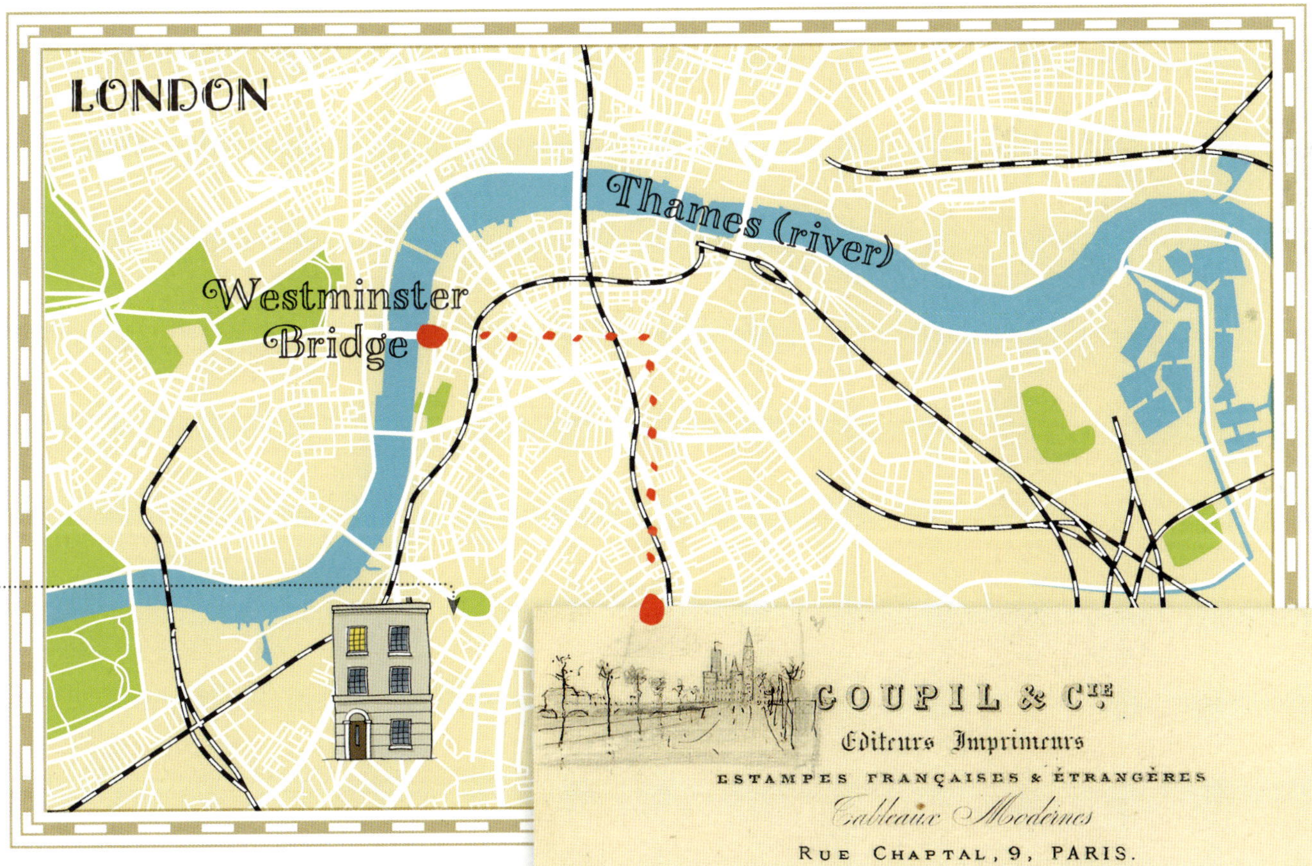

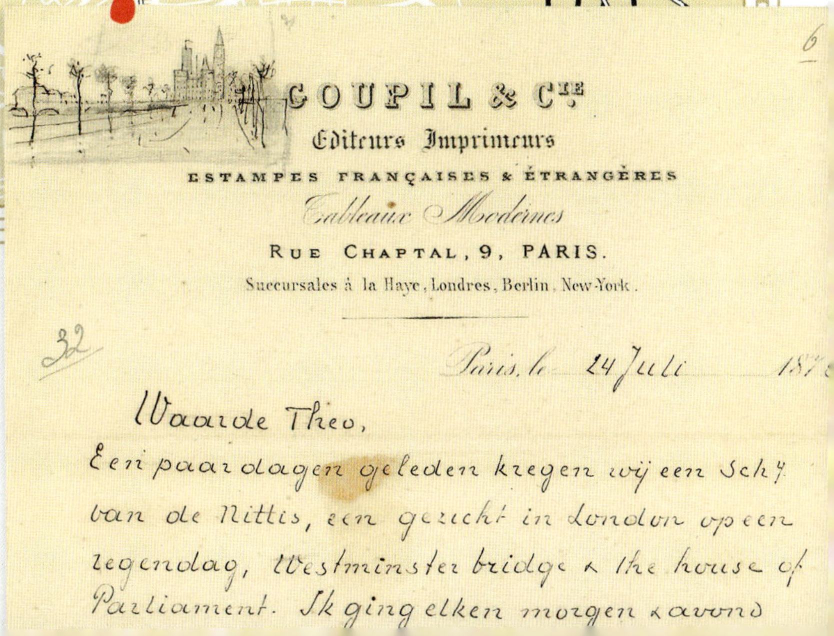
6
GOUPIL & Cie
Éditeurs Imprimeurs
ESTAMPES FRANÇAISES & ÉTRANGÈRES
Tableaux Modernes
RUE CHAPTAL, 9, PARIS.
Succursales à la Haye, Londres, Berlin, New-York.

32

Paris, le 24 Juli 187

Waarde Theo,

Een paar dagen geleden kregen wij een Sch
van de Nittis, een gezicht in London op een
regendag, Westminster bridge & the house of
Parliament. Ik ging elken morgen & avond

Letter from Vincent to Theo, on Goupil stationery. He made a sketch of Westminster Bridge, a bridge over the River Thames in London.

Harry Gladwell, Vincent's friend and work colleague, also had a room in the house in Montmartre, Paris, where Vincent was staying. They read the Bible to each other until late in the evening and fed breadcrumbs to a mouse that lived there.

A LOUER

PARIS
1874–1876

Rooms in Montmartre

In Paris, Vincent had a room in Montmartre, a neighbourhood where lots of artists lived and where there were many cafés and restaurants. But Vincent preferred to return to his room after work. His friend and colleague Harry Gladwell also had a room in the house where Vincent lived. They read to each other from the Bible until late in the evening. Vincent also spent more time writing to Theo. Sometimes Theo received as many as three letters a week from Paris. Vincent's letters became longer and longer. They were increasingly often about God and about the churches Vincent visited in Paris. Vincent thought a lot about how to be a good person. He sometimes copied out entire sections of the Bible in his letters. He thought at the time that it was the only book anyone needed. He even advised Theo to throw away all his other books.

By September, Vincent was already looking forward to Christmas, when he would be able to go home to the Netherlands. He couldn't wait to see Theo again. But when the time came, Vincent's employer wouldn't allow him to take a Christmas holiday. He said they would be too busy. Vincent was stubborn. He went anyway, but that was a bad idea. When he returned to Paris after Christmas, the boss wanted to see him. He was furious, of course, and he fired Vincent. His parents were deeply disappointed. The shame! Their eldest son was already a grown man of twenty-three, and he had lost his job. Whatever was going to become of him?

The beach at Ramsgate.

This was Vincent's view from the boarding school in Ramsgate in 1876.

ENGLAND
1876

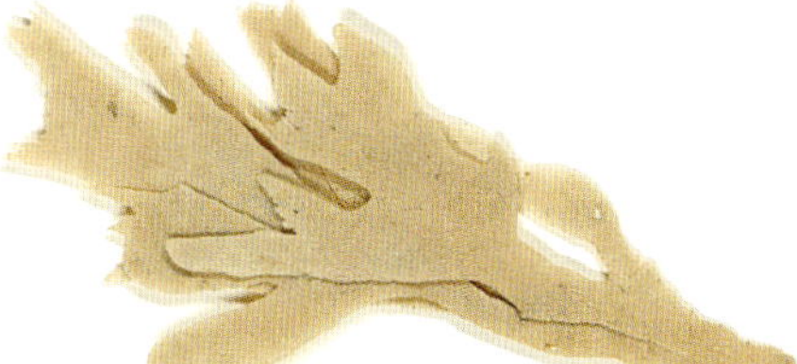

The piece of 'seaweed' from Ramsgate beach that Vincent sent to Theo.

Vincent the teacher

Vincent had had more than enough of the art business. He wanted to do something completely different. We know that he would one day become just about the most famous painter in the world, but he obviously didn't know that himself. He had all kinds of plans after leaving the gallery but not much came of them. He was a teacher at a boarding school in Ramsgate, England, for a while. Actually, he was an assistant teacher, and he didn't earn any money. Here you can see Vincent's drawing of **the view** from this school. You're looking through the same window through which the boys watched their parents as they left them at school. Vincent wrote to Theo that it wasn't a view they would soon forget. He was probably remembering his own time at the boarding school in Zevenbergen and how miserable he felt as his parents drove away in their carriage.

Vincent also worked at another boarding school in England. It was a Christian school in Isleworth, West London, where he was allowed to teach the boys about religion. Vincent loved telling Bible stories in the dormitory. He didn't mind the boys falling asleep, one by one. He was even allowed to preach at a church in Isleworth, just as his father did every Sunday, back home in the Netherlands.

Vincent wrote to his family that what he wanted to do was to help poor people by telling them about religion. He had seen a huge number of people living in slums in the city. If only they started to believe in God, he thought, then maybe they would be at peace with a life of poverty. Vincent's brothers and sisters thought that he was overdoing it with his religion. They called him 'the church trotter' and complained to one another about the long passages from the Bible that he sent to them. 'I believe he is going crazy with religion,' his sister Lies complained in a letter to Theo. Vincent's parents intended to have a serious conversation with him when he was back in the Netherlands. They saw no future in the job at the boarding school in Isleworth and didn't want him to return to England. Was that perhaps a relief for Vincent? We have no way of knowing. In any case, he listened to his parents. He stayed in the Netherlands.

DORDRECHT

1877

The bookshop

Once again, Uncle Cent arranged a job for Vincent. He knew of **a bookshop in Dordrecht** where they could use some help. So, Vincent went to Dordrecht. The job wasn't very exciting. He drew a bit or read the Bible during working hours. Vincent wrote to Theo that he felt miserable about all his failed plans. And he became more and more strict with himself: he did not permit himself to eat meat and he had to read the Bible late into the night. Only then was he finally allowed to go to sleep. On Sundays, he was free, but then he went to three church services, one after the other, at different churches. After church, he went for long walks in the countryside around Dordrecht. As Vincent wandered among the meadows and the water, he remembered how beautiful the Netherlands was – and then he felt happy to be back.

Vincent had three uncles in Amsterdam. When he wanted to study in the city, he was able to stay with his Uncle Jan, who was the director of a naval shipyard, where warships had been built for hundreds of years.

C. M. van Gogh, Keizersgracht 453.
Uncle Cor's shop.
North Sea
Zuiderzee
Amsterdam
IJssel
Dordrecht
Waal
Maas
Etten
UNCLE STRICKER

AMSTERDAM

1877–1878

UNCLE JAN

UNCLE COR

The three uncles

Meanwhile, Vincent was hatching a new plan. He had decided that he wanted to become a minister, like his father. That meant he would have to study for seven years at the University of Amsterdam – and he was already twenty-five. His parents asked him if he was sure. They were afraid that Vincent wouldn't complete his studies. He'd already given up so many times. But Vincent was certain. This was what he wanted.

Luckily, he had no fewer than three uncles in Amsterdam, who were able to give their nephew a little help. To save money, Vincent could stay with **Uncle Jan**, who was the director of the naval shipyard, where warships had been built for hundreds of years. Vincent was given a bedroom and a study. From the window, he looked out at the shipyard, which was full of half-finished ships. At five in the morning, Vincent saw hundreds of labourers streaming through the gate to go to work.

Uncle Stricker, who was also a minister, lived not far from the shipyard. Vincent often went to see him to talk about religion, to have dinner or to drink coffee with his cousins and their friends. They asked him all about his life in Paris and London. Sometimes he stayed until late in the evening. 'You should have been there!' he wrote to Theo the next day.

Vincent also regularly visited **Uncle Cor**, who had a shop selling books and art. He could talk to him about what to read. He was allowed to borrow all kinds of books and **English and French magazines** that he knew from London and Paris. Sometimes he visited Uncle Cor to work his way through an entire stack of these magazines, particularly to look at the pictures.

Walking in Amsterdam

At the time Vincent was living there, Amsterdam was not yet a major city like Paris or London. It was more like a big, sleepy village. Lots of the city's large buildings, such as Centraal Station, the Concertgebouw and the Rijksmuseum, had not yet been built. Vincent went for long walks in Amsterdam too, as he always did when he was in a new place. Then he wrote nice letters to Theo and told him about what he had seen. During his walks in Amsterdam, Vincent spotted all sorts of subjects that would be good for paintings – a girl at the flower market, for instance, or the city by moonlight, or a beautiful old street or a church. Everything reminded him of paintings he knew. But it did not occur to him to paint these subjects himself.

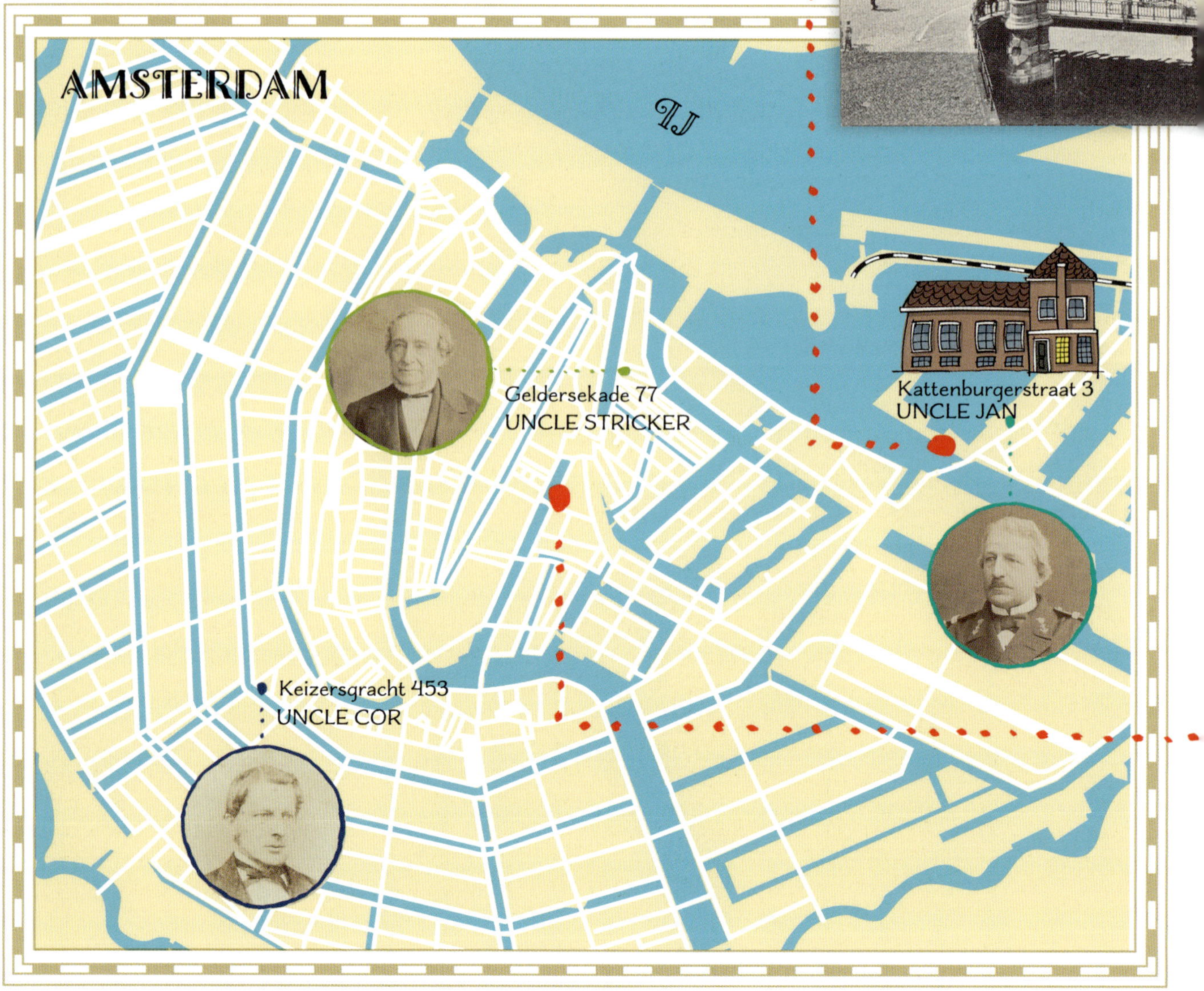

This is where Vincent stayed with his Uncle Jan, on the naval shipyard. The big white building is now the National Maritime Museum.

Vincent walked not only to explore the city, but also to attend as many church services as he could. We know from his letters to Theo that he went to services at ten different churches. Theo sent him some money so that he could visit The Hague one Sunday, but Vincent returned it. He thought it was better for him to go to church as much as possible.

The Trippenhuis on Kloveniersburgwal. Vincent sometimes went there several times a day to look at Rembrandt's paintings.

When he had time, Vincent visited the Trippenhuis, an art museum. Sometimes he went several times a day, to see Rembrandt's paintings. Vincent thought the building was too small for all those works. The paintings were displayed so close together that you couldn't see them properly. It was sometimes very dark as well, and damp, and there was a paraffin stove smoking away. That wasn't very good for the paintings! It was just as well, Vincent wrote to Theo, that there were plans to build a new museum to house them: the Rijksmuseum.

Tutoring

At school, Vincent had studied not only Dutch, but also English, German and French. To become a minister, though, he would have to learn two more languages: **Greek and Latin**. He wrote to Theo about how difficult it was going to be. Luckily, he'd found a tutor for these languages, **Maurits Mendes da Costa**, who was only two years older than Vincent. Vincent thought he was a most remarkable man – maybe even a genius! Vincent started to study hard. He often worked late into the night, memorizing grammar and vocabulary. Sometimes he studied so hard that he saw stars. After a while, he confessed to Theo that he didn't know how he was going to cram it all into his head.

Vincent's tutor Maurits.

It wasn't working. Vincent felt sorry for Maurits because he was such a bad student. So, he took him presents: a book, a drawing, and one time he turned up with a bunch of snowdrops from the park. Maurits watched Vincent struggling for a year. Then he told Uncle Stricker that it would be better for Vincent if he stopped his studies.

Vincent's homework, with notes in Greek.

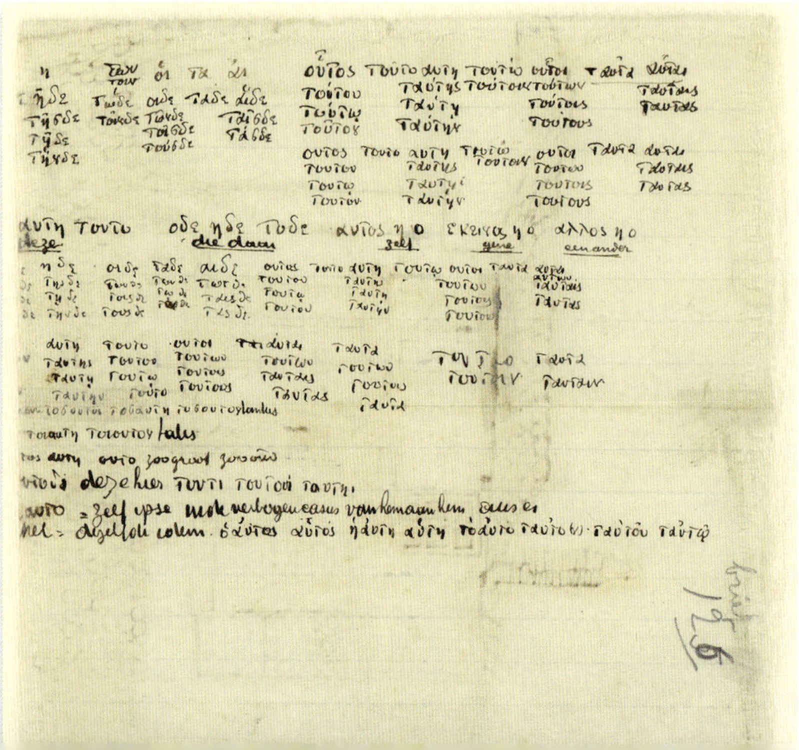

Vincent went back to his parents. They were living in Etten by then, another town in the Dutch province of Brabant. His father had a new job there. Vincent was happy to be home. He went on long walks with his father, and with his brother Cor. They picked heather for the rabbits and drew a map of their walk, which they sent to Theo. Vincent described how beautifully the setting sun shone on the marshes. Looking back, he thought the idea of studying to be a minister for seven years had been a ridiculously bad plan. He believed that living in Amsterdam had been the worst period of his life.

In 1878, Vincent went for a walk in Etten with Cor, his little brother. Together, they drew this map in a letter to Theo.

Vincent had read about the severe poverty in the Borinage, a region in Belgium. He went down into the mines, where he saw the emaciated workers and seven old horses that did the heavy work.

North Sea
The Hague
Netherlands
AU PECHEUR
Bruxelles
Le marché Ste Catherine.
Nels, Bruxelles Serie 1 Nr. 201
Belgium
Brussels
BORINAGE
Hornu Charbonnage d'Hornu-Wasmes No 4.
France

THE BORINAGE (BELGIUM)

1878–1880

The dangerous Marcasse mine.

Drawing

After his miserable stay in Amsterdam, Vincent embarked upon a different course of study – in Brussels this time, where there was a three-year course to become a minister, and you didn't have to learn Greek and Latin. But that didn't turn out well either. Vincent decided that he would never start another course of study again. This time, though, he didn't return home. He had read about the extreme poverty in the Borinage. This was an area of Belgium **where coal was taken from the ground** to be used as fuel to heat houses and to power steam trains. Miners with lamps on their heads were sent down in cages to extract coal with pickaxes, 700 metres below the surface. It was hard and risky work, and they earned very little money. The miners lived in poverty. Even without a qualification and without Greek and Latin, Vincent thought he would be able to do good work there. When he arrived in the Borinage, he wanted to see what it was like inside a mine, so he went down with the workers into the dangerous Marcasse mine. Men regularly died down there because of gas explosions, floods and cave-ins. Vincent thought it was like being lowered into a well in a bucket. When he looked up, the daylight seemed like a little star in the sky. Down below, he saw the emaciated miners: men, women, children. There were also seven old horses that transported larger amounts of coal. He felt very sorry for them.

The black sheep

In the village of Wasmes, Vincent had a job as an assistant minister: he read from the Bible, taught the children and took care of the sick. He even gave away his own coat and blankets. His bosses were impressed by Vincent's love for the poor. But an assistant minister should also be good at telling stories – and they were not impressed by Vincent's storytelling skills. So, they looked for someone else for the job. Vincent could not believe it. What was he supposed to do now? He was already twenty-six, and he'd lost another job. He had become the family's problem child, the 'black sheep', and everyone had an opinion about what he should do with his life. One of them suggested that Vincent should work for a printer. Another thought he would make a good carpenter. His sister Anna even believed he should become a baker. Imagine if the world's most famous painter had listened to his sister!

Vincent's drawing of miners walking through the snow to work, 1880.

Vincent was furious. If the whole family thought he was useless, then he had better just stay away from them. He didn't want to return to Etten. But the truth was that he didn't know what to do either. So, for a while, he didn't do anything. He read books and **did a drawing now and then**. He found a place to live with a very poor family in the village of Cuesmes, also in the Borinage, where he shared a bedroom with the children. Sometimes he had no money for weeks. Sometimes his father sent him some cash.

Vincent's parents had no idea what was going to become of him. They sent Theo to Belgium to talk to Vincent, but the brothers argued. They did not write each other any letters for a year. But Theo did not forget his brother. He now had a good job at Goupil in Paris and, after a while, he sent Vincent some **money**. Vincent replied with a long, eight-page letter to thank his brother and to explain how he felt. Then the two of them were friends again.

Vincent's watercolour of a coke factory in the Borinage, 1879.

Learning to draw

At some point during this period, Vincent had a flash of intuition. He was not an art dealer, not a schoolteacher and not a minister. Could he perhaps be an *artist*? Maybe he should start drawing the lives of the miners. If English and French magazines would print his drawings, he could show the readers what hard lives the miners had, how poor they were, and how unfair it all was! If he sold his work, he would finally be able to earn his own money again. Then he would no longer have to rely on his parents or Theo.

It seemed like a good plan. To start with, he would have to learn how to draw very well, Vincent wrote to Theo. He needed to practise his drawing. He worked late into the night. He spent time reading anatomy books, which showed how the human body works. He also did exercises in the techniques of depth and perspective, which make it possible for artists to create drawings that look as if you could step right into them.

Vincent had no time to write long letters now, but he could still write short ones. He asked Theo to send him prints to copy – as soon as possible! Vincent also asked Mr Tersteeg, his old boss, if he could borrow the books with drawing lessons that were in the gallery in The Hague. Mr Tersteeg sent not only books, but also – much to Vincent's surprise – a box of paints and a sketchbook. Vincent immediately did all the exercises in the book, one after the other. He called his drawings awkward 'scratches' for some time. But suddenly he realized that he was making progress. His 'scratches' were getting better and better. He wrote to Theo that he hoped they would soon improve even more – because he was already twenty-seven and he had no time to lose.

Vincent practised copying prints that Theo sent to him. This one was based on a **print by the French artist Jean-François Millet.**

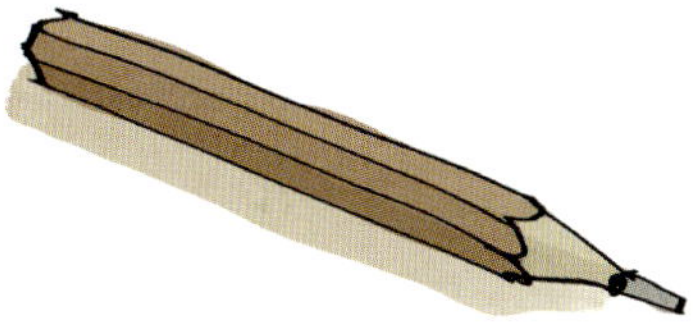

BRUSSELS
1880–1881

Now that Vincent was becoming an artist, he could not stand to remain in the Borinage any longer. The people there had never even seen a painting! Vincent wanted to visit museums and to talk to other artists. He looked for a room in Brussels and even enrolled for another course of study. It was at an art school this time, where you could take free classes. But it was not a good decision: he had to draw boring plaster sculptures all day long. What Vincent really wanted to do was to practise with real people! He didn't find the other first-year students interesting to talk to either. They were all ten years younger than he was.

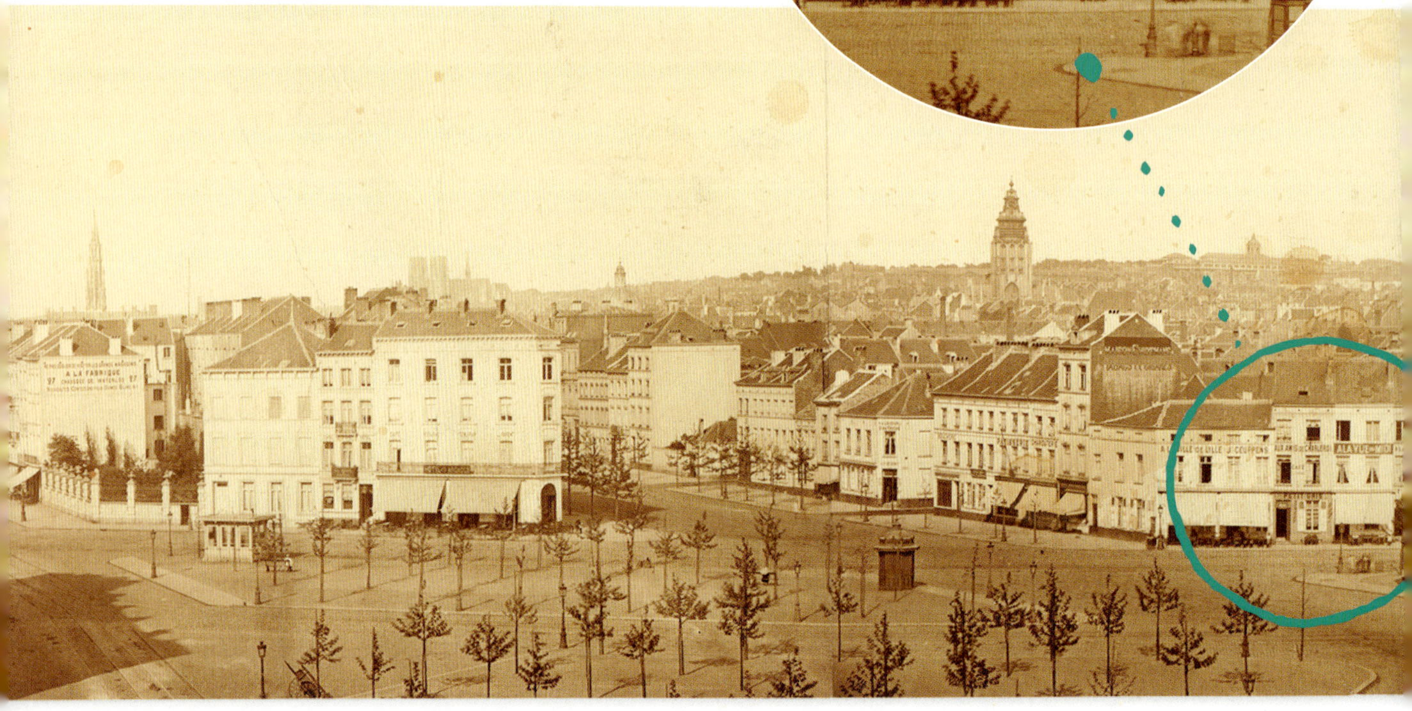

Vincent did know an interesting person though: another Dutch artist. His name was **Anthon van Rappard**, and his drawing skills were more advanced than Vincent's. Anthon had a large studio in Brussels all to himself, a space where he could work on his art. He let Vincent come and work there now and then. Vincent could not afford a studio of his own. His father gave him sixty francs a month, but the rent for his room was already fifty francs. He had to use the rest to buy food, paper, drawing equipment, prints, clothes and new shoes. He also had to pay his models, the people who were willing to pose so that he could draw them. Everything was more expensive in Brussels than it had been in the Borinage. Luckily, Theo offered to send Vincent money until he was able to earn some for himself again. He also invited his brother to come and live with him in Paris. However, Vincent thought it was all going a bit too fast. He decided first to spend a summer with their parents, in Etten.

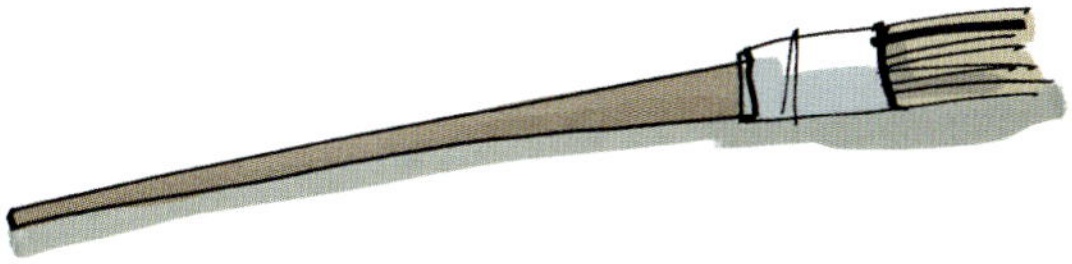

Vincent rented a room in this building, opposite the station in Brussels.

North Sea
Zuiderzee
Hoogeveen
Amsterdam
The Hague
IJssel
Netherlands
Waal
Maas
Rhine
Etten
Nuenen
Belgium
Brussels

ETTEN
1881

The house where Vincent's parents lived, with his studio next to it. Vincent drew the house in 1876, when he was not yet an artist.

A studio of his own

In Etten, Vincent had **a studio of his own** for the first time. It was in a small building by the house where his parents lived. Sometimes he worked so hard that he didn't hear his mother calling that the coffee was ready. He thought eating was a waste of time. He had to keep working. The walls of the studio were soon covered with drawings. Vincent often worked outside too, in and around Etten. He was a familiar figure in the village. Carrying all his painting equipment under his arm, he walked down the street in his raincoat, or he sat sketching on the roadside. He had no time for a chat when he was working. He preferred to draw people when they were working on the land, but he also visited them at home. It was hard to explain to them how to pose, he complained in a letter to Theo in Paris. Vincent wanted to draw them in their work clothes, while they were doing their jobs. But when the people of Etten knew that Vincent was coming to visit, they wore their Sunday best. After all, he was the minister's son. In the summer, Vincent's friend Anthon came to Etten. He stayed for two weeks. The two friends took their folding chairs out into the countryside, to the heath and the marshes, to draw and paint landscapes. They also had long conversations about art.

ANTON

Good news

From Etten, Vincent travelled to The Hague for a few days. He showed his work to his old boss, Mr Tersteeg, at Goupil, who thought that Vincent was making progress. He also visited **Anton Mauve**'s beautiful studio. Mauve was a famous painter, who happened to be married to one of Vincent's cousins. His landscapes were popular and were also sold abroad. Mauve was a member of the 'Hague School', a group of artists who painted Dutch landscapes. They mainly used dark colours, as that was what people in the Netherlands were used to. Mauve thought Vincent's drawings were interesting. He also said that he should try working with oil paints. They agreed that Vincent would soon return to show him his new work. As soon as he was back in Etten, Vincent wrote Theo a letter to tell him about all the positive reactions. Now that he was becoming a real artist, he should indeed start working with oil paints. He was ready. Much to his surprise, following his visit, his cousin Mauve sent him a box of painting equipment, including oil paint, brushes and all the other equipment that a real artist needs.

Sketches in a letter to Theo from the town of Etten, 1881.

Boy with a Sickle, 1881

KEE and her son.

The family drama

Vincent's cousin Kee Vos also came to stay in Etten that summer, along with her young son. Kee was the daughter of Uncle Stricker, the uncle who had helped Vincent when he was studying to become a minister in Amsterdam. Kee's husband had died, and she was still very sad. Vincent and Kee got along well with each other, but then Vincent fell in love with her. Out of the blue, he asked her to marry him. Kee's answer was clear: 'No, nay, never.' But Vincent thought he could persuade her. So, after she returned home, he started to write her long letters. Vincent's parents wanted him to stop writing these dramatic letters. After a huge argument with his parents, he caught the train to Amsterdam, so that he could talk to Kee himself. Vincent thought he was being clever – he called at the Strickers' home at dinnertime. But Kee was not there. He kept trying, but he did not get to see her. Vincent even went as far as to hold his hand in the flame of an oil lamp, just to show how much he wanted to see Kee. But, of course, someone blew out the flame. Uncle Stricker, who saw it all happen, was so angry that he almost began to swear. Almost.

Anton Mauve's studio was on this canal in The Hague.

THE HAGUE

1881–1883

Rijnspoor Station in 1875. Now called The Hague Central Station.

Thrown out

Vincent did not feel like returning to his parents after this family drama. So, he took **the train to The Hague** and went to visit Anton Mauve again. He asked if he could study with him for a few weeks. Anton agreed and put his cousin to work. He told Vincent to make a still life: a pot with a spoon in it, with a bottle, a crumpled cloth and a pair of clogs. It was Vincent's **first work made with oil paints**.

Vincent's first oil painting: *Still Life with Clogs*, 1881

Vincent did not go to see his parents again until it was almost Christmas. That visit also ended in an argument. He wrote to Theo that he had never been so angry before. It all started when he said that he did not want to go to church with his parents. In fact, he wanted nothing more to do with religion. This turned into such a quarrel that his father threw him out of the house. Vincent went straight back to The Hague, where he received an angry letter from Theo. His brother wanted to know why on earth Vincent had acted so childishly and made Pa and Ma's life so miserable. However, he still went on sending money, so that Vincent could continue to paint.

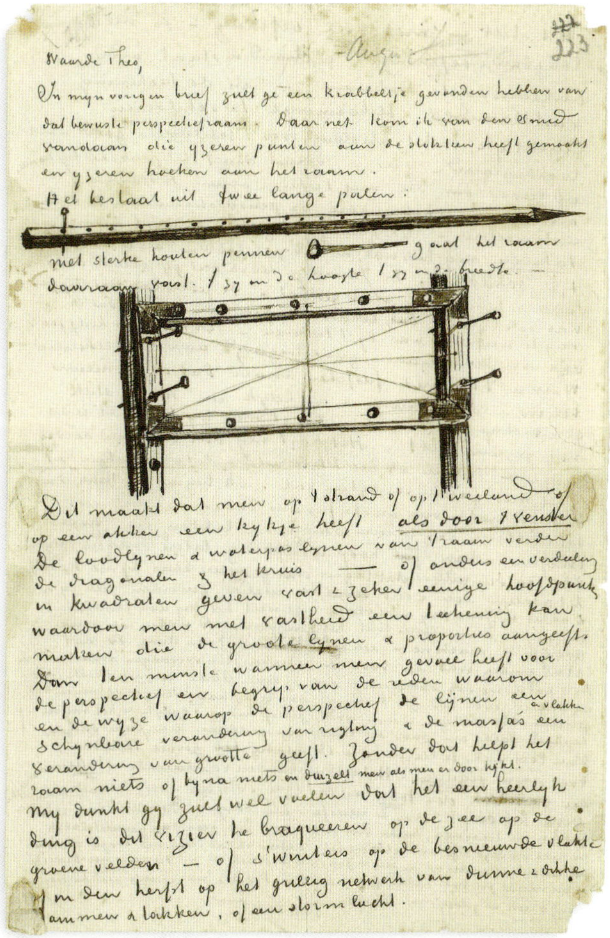
Waarde Theo,
In mijn vorigen brief zult ge een krabbeltje gevonden hebben van dat bewuste perspectiefraam. Daar net kom ik van den smid vandaan die ijzeren punten aan de stokken heeft gemaakt en ijzeren hoeken aan het raam.
Het bestaat uit twee lange palen:
met sterke houten pennen gaat het raam daaraan vast.
Dit maakt dat men op 't strand of op 't weiland of op een akker een kijkje heeft als door 't venster. De loodlijnen & waterpaslijnen van 't raam verder de diagonalen & het kruis — of anders een verdeeling in kwadraten geven vast & zeker eenige hoofdpunten waardoor men met vastheid een teekening kan maken die de groote lijnen & proporties aangeeft. Dan ten minste wanneer men gevoel heeft voor de perspectief en begrip van de reden waarom de perspectief de lijnen een schijnbare verandering van rigting & de massa's een verandering van grootte geeft. Zonder dat helpt het raam niets of bijna niets en duizelt men als men er door kijkt.
Mij dunkt gij zult wel voelen dat het een heerlijk ding is dit vizier te braqueeren op de zee op de groene velden — of 's winters op de besneeuwde vlakte of in den herfst op het grillig netwerk van dunne & dikke takken, of een stormlucht.

Work for Uncle Cor

In The Hague, Vincent found a cheap house on the edge of the city. It was his first real house – and he had it all to himself! He bought chairs, a sturdy kitchen table and even boxes of flower bulbs. Then he got down to work. He wrote to Theo that he really loved drawing, just like a sailor loves the sea.

On his walks around the city, Vincent drew the buildings he saw, using pencil, ink and white watercolour paint. To his surprise, Uncle Cor, the one with the art and book shop in Amsterdam, bought three of his drawings – for two guilders fifty each! That was quite a lot of money at the time. Then Uncle Cor ordered another twelve of these 'townscapes'. 'Theo, it's almost miraculous!!!' – that was what Vincent wrote to his brother, complete with three exclamation marks.

When he was making these townscapes, Vincent was able to practise drawing the right perspective. Vincent found it difficult, and it didn't always work out well, as you can see on page 65. The men at the front look larger than the people who are more in the distance, as they would in real life. However, they are so big that they look like giants. They don't fit into the space. Vincent was annoyed that it hadn't worked. Why hadn't he been taught how to do this at school? So, he read books about perspective and even asked a carpenter to make **a device** that would help him to get the perspective right.

A letter to Theo written in 1882, with a sketch of the device that Vincent got someone to make for him: a perspective frame.

THE HAGUE

Townscapes that Vincent made in 1882 in The Hague.

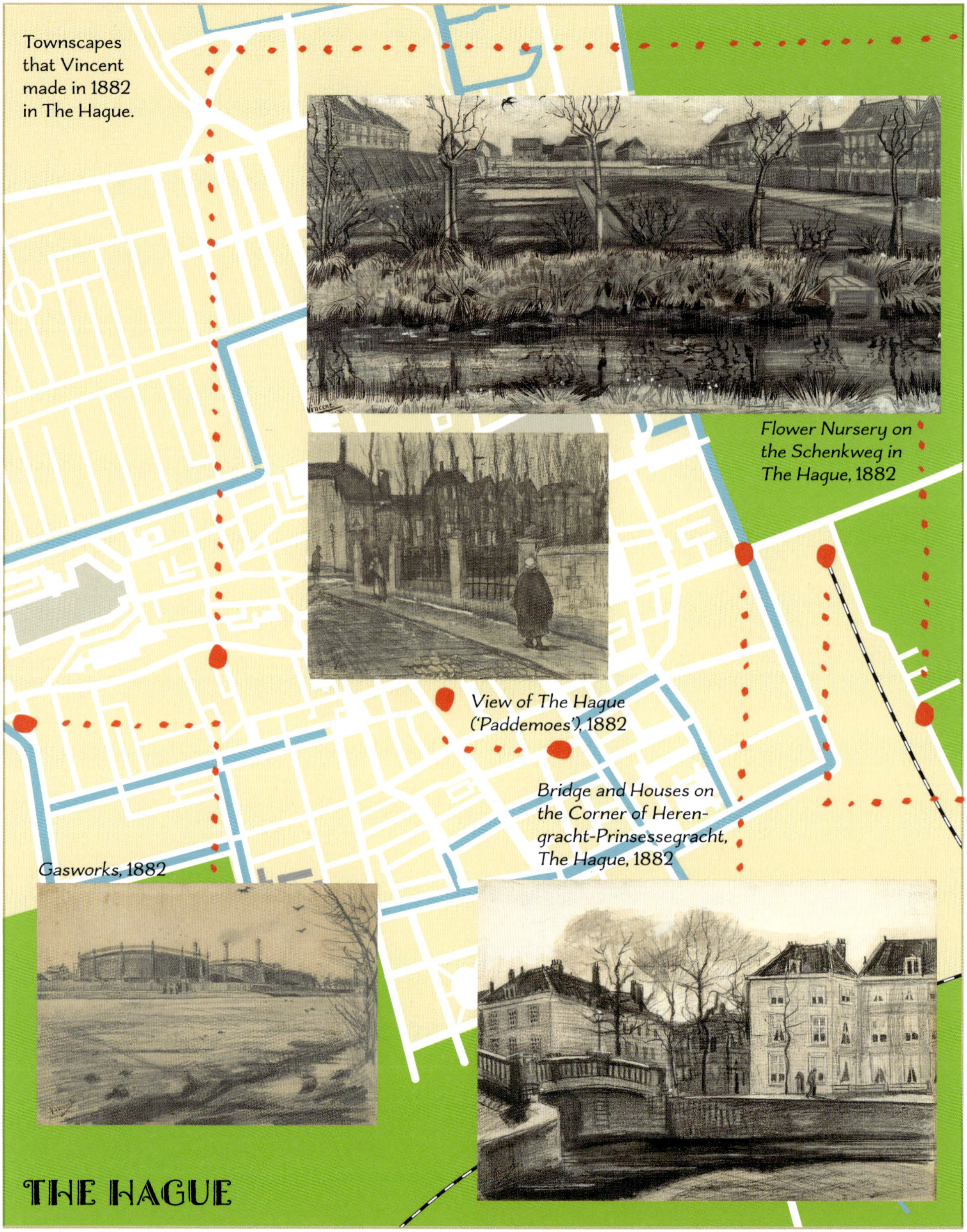

Flower Nursery on the Schenkweg in The Hague, 1882

View of The Hague ('Paddemoes'), 1882

Bridge and Houses on the Corner of Herengracht-Prinsessegracht, The Hague, 1882

Gasworks, 1882

The Entrance to the Pawn Bank, The Hague, 1882

Here you can see that Vincent had problems with the perspective. The people at the front look like giants. He drew them far too big.

Staatsspoor Station, 1882
Rijnspoor Station, near Vincent's house.

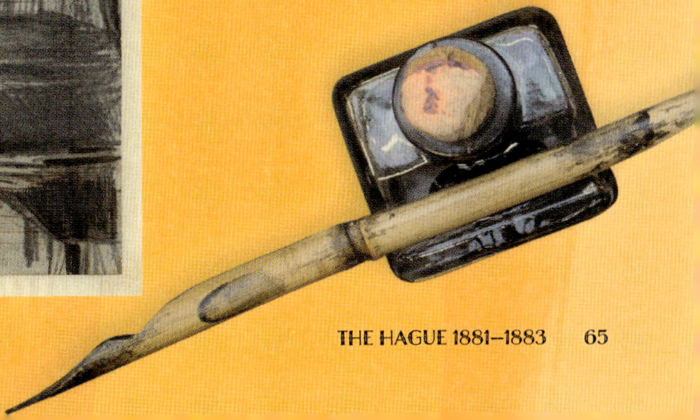

View from Vincent's studio: *Carpenter's Yard and Laundry*, 1882

Sien

Anton Mauve thought Vincent needed more practice at drawing people. However, not many people wanted to pose for him. Some didn't show up, while others asked for too much money. When he didn't have a model, Vincent went to sketch in places where there were a lot of people. Like a railway station, for example, or a soup kitchen, where poor people came to eat. That was how he met Sien Hoornik. She often modelled for Vincent. **Sien had a five-year-old daughter** and was expecting a second child. However, she did not have a husband. In Vincent's day, a lot of people thought that was a disgrace. When Vincent met Sien, she was ill and very poor. He made sure she started eating well and that she went to hospital so that she could get better. Vincent wanted to look after her and her children and to live with Sien. He wrote to Theo that he even wanted to marry her. Theo was not enthusiastic about Vincent living with an ordinary working-class woman. And marrying her? That was going too far. Their parents could not understand Vincent choosing a woman from a poor family either. But Vincent persevered. Who else was going to look after Sien and her children?

Sien and her daughter: *Woman with a Child on Her Lap*, 1883

Floorplan of the house where Vincent lived with Sien and her children.

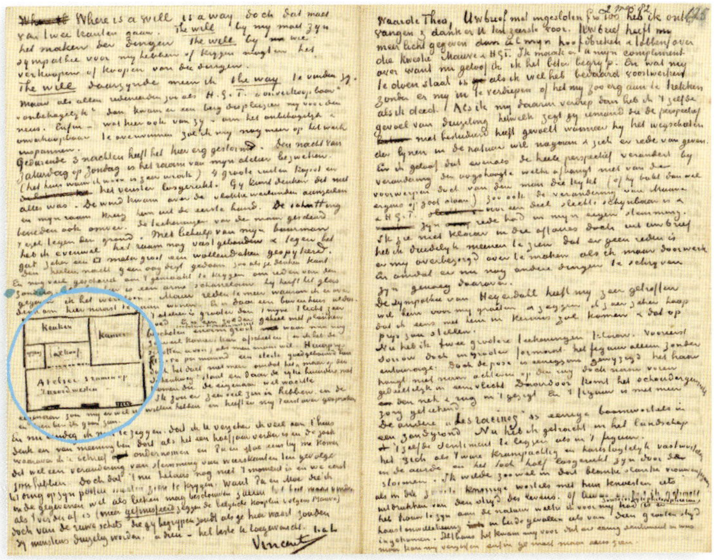

Sien's daughter and son:
Girl Kneeling by a Cradle, 1882

Family man

Now Vincent suddenly had a family. **He did wonderful drawings of Sien and her children**. It seemed like a fairy tale, but unfortunately it did not last very long. That was because of Sien's mother and brother. Vincent thought they were a bad influence on her and that she should have no contact with them. However, Sien secretly went to visit her family. After a furious argument, Vincent said that they should break up. He cancelled the rent on their house and decided that he would continue with his painting elsewhere. Sien and her children came to say goodbye to Vincent at the station. He wrote to Theo that it was not an easy farewell, but that it was better if he left.

A turf hut in Drenthe.

A Peat Barge with Two Figures, 1883

Peat

In Drenthe, lots of people made their money from peat. Peat is made of the remains of compressed marsh plants. There are thick layers of it in the ground, and it burns well when it's dry. It was a common fuel in Vincent's day, not only for the stove at home, but also in factories. Peat workers dug it up by hand.

Turning the peat in Drenthe, 1900–1920.
This made it easier for the blocks of peat to dry. Women and children worked with the peat too. The youngest children sat on the blocks and watched.

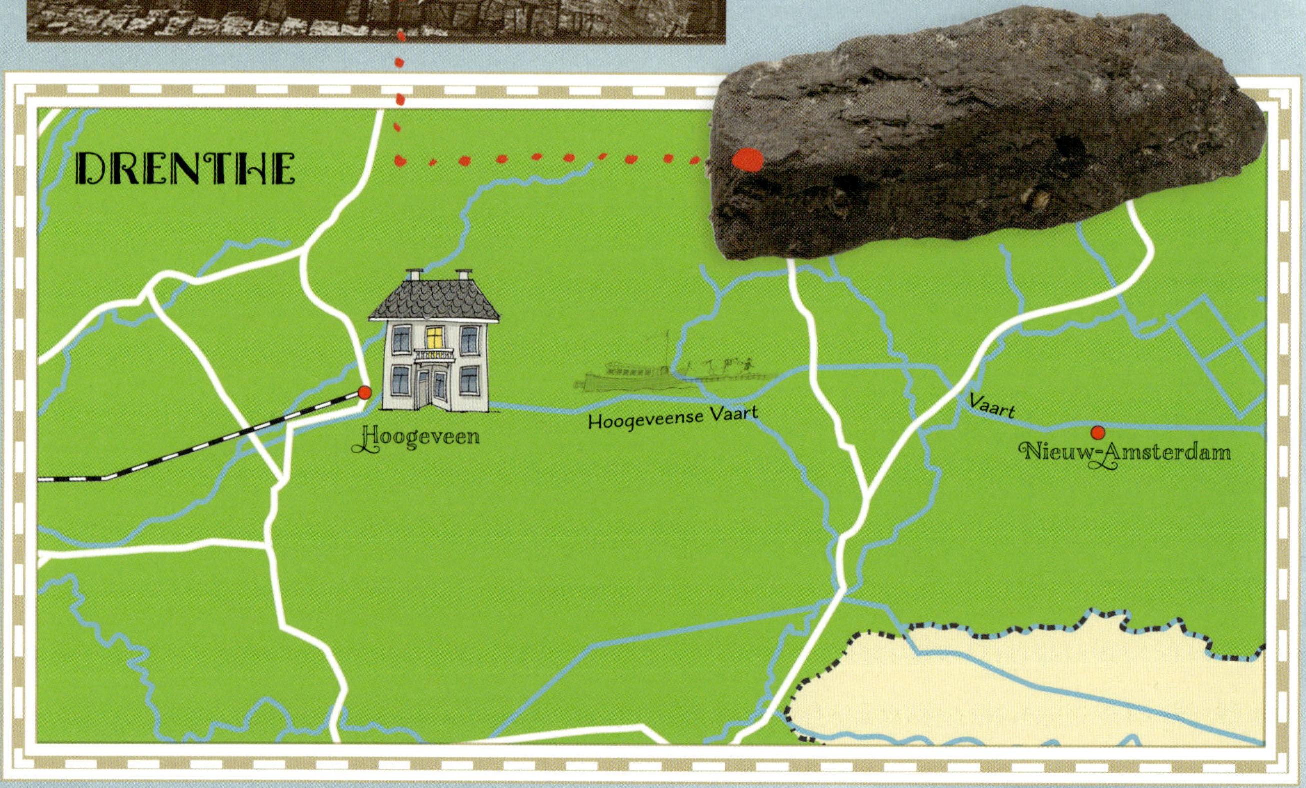

DRENTHE

1883

Hoogeveen

Vincent had wanted to visit the Dutch province of Drenthe for some time. That was because of his friend Anthon van Rappard, who had written him letters telling him about all the beautiful subjects that there were to paint in Drenthe. After a long journey, Vincent arrived in Hoogeveen in the dark. He rented a room at a hotel and couldn't wait for it to become light. He was so eager to go out walking in the surrounding countryside. And he was not disappointed – he found absolutely everything beautiful in Drenthe. He wrote to Theo that it was even more beautiful than Brabant. There were so many subjects to draw and paint! Like the turf huts, for example, which were low houses with heather and grass on the roof instead of tiles. One day, when Vincent wanted to paint one of these huts, he saw a goat and two sheep jump onto the roof to graze. The woman who lived there came running out with a broom to chase them away. She obviously didn't want them to eat her roof. Vincent's letters to Theo are packed with drawings of peat workers doing their job. They often wore short trousers. This allowed Vincent to study their legs and movements closely so that he could copy them. Unfortunately, the locals did not want to pose for Vincent. 'People laughed about it, and I was ridiculed,' he wrote to Theo. It was time to move on.

Sketches that Vincent made in Drenthe in 1883.

A peat barge on a canal in Hoogeveen.

Nieuw-Amsterdam

And so Vincent went on a tow barge to the village of Nieuw-Amsterdam. Barges like this were pulled by a horse and sometimes even by people, who walked along the side of the water. The journey was thirty kilometres. For Vincent, it felt like an eternity. Luckily, he soon found a room where he could live. But most of the time he was outside, because he thought everything in Nieuw-Amsterdam was even more beautiful than in Hoogeveen. Vincent sometimes walked dozens of kilometres a day. He described everything in detail to Theo, in long letters full of sketches. Vincent tried to persuade his brother to come and paint in Drenthe. But Theo declared that he most definitely did not want to become a painter. He didn't come to Drenthe. Vincent had no family nearby, and no friends. After a few weeks, he began to feel really lonely in Drenthe. And then the weather turned bad, too. It was too wet to paint outside. Vincent became ill. One stormy afternoon, in the rain and snow, he walked for six hours across the heath to Hoogeveen, where he got on the train. He wanted to go home. To Brabant.

In Nuenen, Vincent spent a lot of time practising his art at the home of the De Groots, a farming family. He made dozens of sketches and practice paintings.

The Van Gogh family's home in Nuenen, with Vincent's studio in the large shed.

Long live the paint tube

Vincent preferred to paint outside. But that had some disadvantages, such as insects flying into your work. Some of these insects are still stuck in the paint on his paintings. Grains of sand and tiny stones also got blown onto the paint, or sometimes the canvas got scratched, perhaps by swishing branches. But Vincent didn't care about any of that.

The invention of the paint tube had made it possible to paint outside in Vincent's day. If Vincent had lived fifty years earlier, he would have had to carry around homemade paint in pigs' bladders or glass tubes. That wasn't very convenient. Paint dries out quickly in bladders, and glass tubes are fragile. That was why the painters who came before Vincent preferred to stay in their studios. The invention of these tin tubes with screw tops allowed oil paint to be stored safely for a long time. You could buy it in all kinds of different colours as well. That meant that painters like Vincent no longer had to worry about using too much paint, as the artists before them had done. When they ran out of paint, they could just go and buy a few more tubes.

NUENEN
1883–1885

The back garden in Nuenen:
Garden of the Rectory at Nuenen, 1885

The shaggy dog

Vincent's parents no longer lived in Etten. They had moved to another village, still in the province of Brabant: Nuenen. His father was the minister there. Vincent's twenty-one-year-old sister Willemien and his sixteen-year-old brother Cor still lived at home. They must have been a little surprised when their thirty-year-old brother came home. He was wearing a peasant's smock, a big hairy coat and a fur hat. It was not exactly what a minister's son was supposed to look like. Vincent hoped to find a little peace in Nuenen. But things went wrong between him and his parents again. They had another argument. Disappointed, Vincent wrote to Theo that 'nothing, nothing, nothing' about their father and the situation at home had changed. His parents treated him like a big, shaggy dog who walked around the house with dirty, wet paws, getting in their way and barking all the time. However, he stayed in Nuenen, partly because it was cheaper to live at home. His parents had a shed emptied for Vincent to use as a studio. He threw himself into his work. As he was annoyed that he had to keep asking Theo for money, he came to an agreement with his brother. In exchange for the money, Vincent would give Theo all the work that he made. Theo could do whatever he wanted with it. His brother agreed to this plan. From then on, Vincent sent him parcels and boxes of drawings and paintings. Sometimes the paint wasn't even dry when the paintings arrived in Paris.

Weavers and farmworkers

Vincent wanted to draw the miners in the Borinage. In Drenthe, it was the peat workers. Hardworking people – that was what he was always looking for. In Nuenen, he found the weavers. These people had looms at home, which they used to weave metres of fabric by hand. They were huge machines, and they made a terrible noise. They were almost too big to fit into the weavers' small houses. Vincent visited their homes and drew them while they were hard at work. It took him a while to figure out how to draw the complicated machines. He wrote to Theo that the weavers and their wives had to work for hours on end and that they earned very little money.

Some other hard workers in Nuenen were the smallholders. Vincent often went to visit them, too. Smallholders did not make enough money with their own little farms, so they also used to work on the land of wealthy local farmers.

In one of Vincent's sketchbooks, you can see that **he kept practising how to draw the postures of working people**. They posed for him holding a shovel or a pitchfork, as if they were working. Vincent had better luck with models in Nuenen than he had in Drenthe. Some of them even came to his studio to pose. But the studio was a bit too small. And having his parents around all the time became a little too much for Vincent. So, he rented another room in Nuenen, where he could work in the daytime.

And then something very sad happened: Vincent's father died unexpectedly. Vincent sent a telegram to Theo in Paris, and Theo travelled to Nuenen for the funeral as quickly as he could. It was an unhappy time, but Vincent soon went back to work, which annoyed his sister Anna. She had stayed in Nuenen to look after their mother. She thought that Vincent should think a little more about other people, not just himself. Vincent wasn't going to put up with her saying that, of course. After an argument, he went to live in his studio. He wrote to Theo that it was better for everyone.

Sketches of People Working in the Fields, 1884–1885

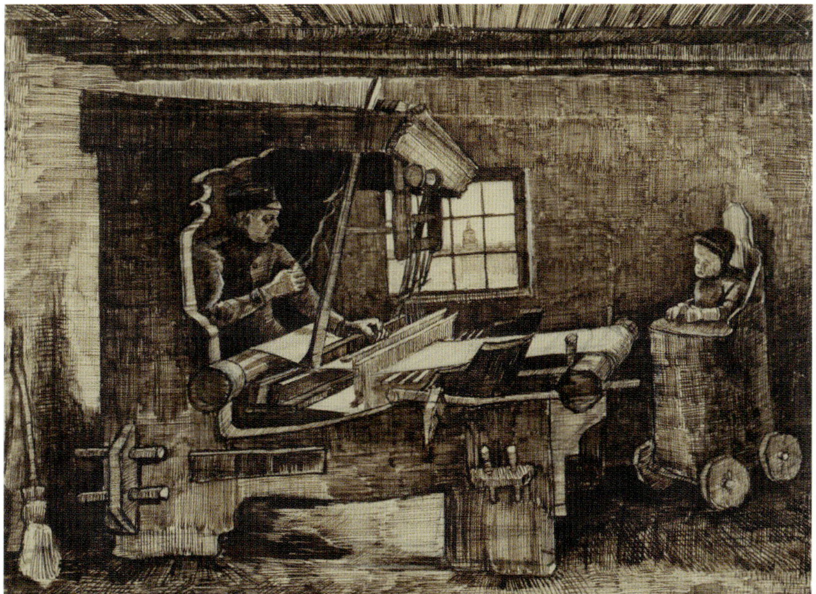

Drawing from 1884 of a weaver at a loom. Do you see the baby in the highchair?

The Potato Eaters

Meanwhile, Vincent was thinking hard about a special painting that he wanted to make. It was going to be a large work, with a lot of people in it. He'd already spent some time practising at the home of the De Groots, a peasant family. **He made portraits of Gordina, wearing her big white hat**, and of the rest of the family too. **He drew hands holding a fork** or a cup of coffee. He also drew the clock on the wall, the oil lamp, the cat and the door. Vincent made dozens of sketches and practice paintings, sometimes with four people at the dinner table, sometimes with five. Then he finally started work on the actual painting. He worked on it for a month. When it was finished, Vincent thought it had turned out really well. He wanted Theo to submit it for an important exhibition or to sell it. He even copied the painting onto a special sort of stone, so that he could have prints made of it. He would send the print to well-known painters to show them what he'd made. And Theo would be able to show the **print** to art dealers in Paris. Maybe a magazine would like to print the drawing?

Vincent sent this print to his friend Anthon.

These are sketches of Gordina from 1884-1885.

Vincent spent a lot of time practising how to paint faces. Gordina was the model for this practice piece in oil paints. This study is called:
Head of a Woman (Gordina de Groot), 1885

Sketch of Three Hands, Two Holding Forks, 1885

The Potato Eaters, 1885

The reactions

The Potato Eaters is now one of the most famous paintings in the world, but when it had just been finished, hardly anyone liked it. Vincent's friend Anthon van Rappard thought Vincent could do better. He didn't really intend it as a serious painting, did he? Anthon wrote Vincent a letter, listing everything that he thought was wrong with it. He pointed out a hand that was badly painted, an arm that was far too short, and someone who was missing a knee. The nose of one of the women looked like a pipe stem with a cube on the end, he said. Vincent was furious. As far as he was concerned, the friendship was over. He returned Anthon's letter. They never saw each other again.

Unfortunately, Theo wasn't very enthusiastic either. He thought the painting was far too dark. It was much too old-fashioned for the spoiled art lovers of Paris. Vincent saw his point. But he didn't entirely agree. He thought he had painted the real life of peasants. *The Potato Eaters* remained his favourite painting for some time.

Leaving Brabant

Of course, the time came when Vincent wanted to leave Brabant too. After almost two years, he'd had enough of Nuenen. Gordina de Groot, one of the potato eaters, was pregnant. People in the village suspected that Vincent was the father. That wasn't true, Vincent wrote to Theo. However, it still caused him a lot of problems. The priest of the Catholic church in the village told the locals to stop posing for Vincent. That meant he no longer had any models in Nuenen, which was a good reason to move on again. Vincent wanted to paint for a while in Antwerp. He left most of his work behind, thinking he would fetch it later. He often thought back to Brabant. However, he would never return there.

In Antwerp, Vincent did what he always did when he was in a new city: he went out for a long walk. Everywhere he went, he saw interesting people, including sailors, a Chinese girl, and dockers with big muscles.

ANTWERP

The port in Antwerp.

The art academy in Antwerp.

ANTWERP
1885–1886

The art academy

In Antwerp, Vincent did what he always did whenever he was in a new city: he went for a long walk. A city was quite different from the sand, the heath and the tranquillity of a country village, Vincent wrote to Theo. He went to the museum, and to churches and **dance halls**. At the port, he walked along the quaysides, where ships were being unloaded. He saw interesting people everywhere he went: sailors, a Chinese girl, and dockers with big muscles. But living in a city also had disadvantages. Everything was more expensive – painting equipment for one thing, and models.

A dance hall in Antwerp, 1885. Vincent made these sketches with red and blue crayons.

Couple Dancing, 1885

Two Women in a Balcony Box, 1885

Dance Hall, 1885

The Discus Thrower, 1886

View of Het Steen, 1886

Vincent thought he had a good idea: he applied to study at the art academy. The lessons were free, and he hoped there would be models there to draw. But the director made Vincent start by **practising drawing plaster sculptures**. That was also interesting, but it wasn't what he wanted to do. He didn't last long on this course either. He wrote to Theo that he thought the other students' work was 'hopelessly bad'. And he told them so, too. It was hardly surprising that he didn't make any friends in Antwerp.

The room of plaster sculptures at the academy and a sketch by Vincent. Do you see the sculpture that Vincent copied during his lesson?

Hunger

Painting equipment and models were so expensive that Vincent had no money left for food. Feeling faint with hunger, Vincent sat drawing **a famous castle** in Antwerp. He hoped to sell a painting of the castle as a souvenir. But no one was interested in his work. Fortunately, Theo continued to send money, for which Vincent was very grateful. But he didn't use the money for food. He spent it on hiring a model. Things were clearly not going to end well. Vincent ate so infrequently in Antwerp that his stomach stopped working properly. He smoked a lot, so that he wouldn't feel the hunger – and that made him cough. One tooth after another fell out. The doctor told Vincent to start living more healthily. So, he tried to slow down. He ate a few times a day and went to bed earlier. He saw the dentist. Vincent slowly recovered. And one day he decided it was time for a change again. Vincent caught the train to Paris. He was going to Theo.

PARIS
1886–1888

Boulevard Montmartre in Paris.

In Paris

Vincent arrived in Paris early in the morning. He had **a note** delivered to Theo, saying that they should meet in the Louvre Museum at twelve. We do not know if they actually met there, though. Vincent then shared a house with Theo for about two years. For a while, they had no need to write each other letters. That is unfortunate for us, as Vincent's work changed dramatically during his time in Paris. It would be interesting to find out more about what Vincent was doing at the time, what he talked to Theo about, and which famous artists he met.

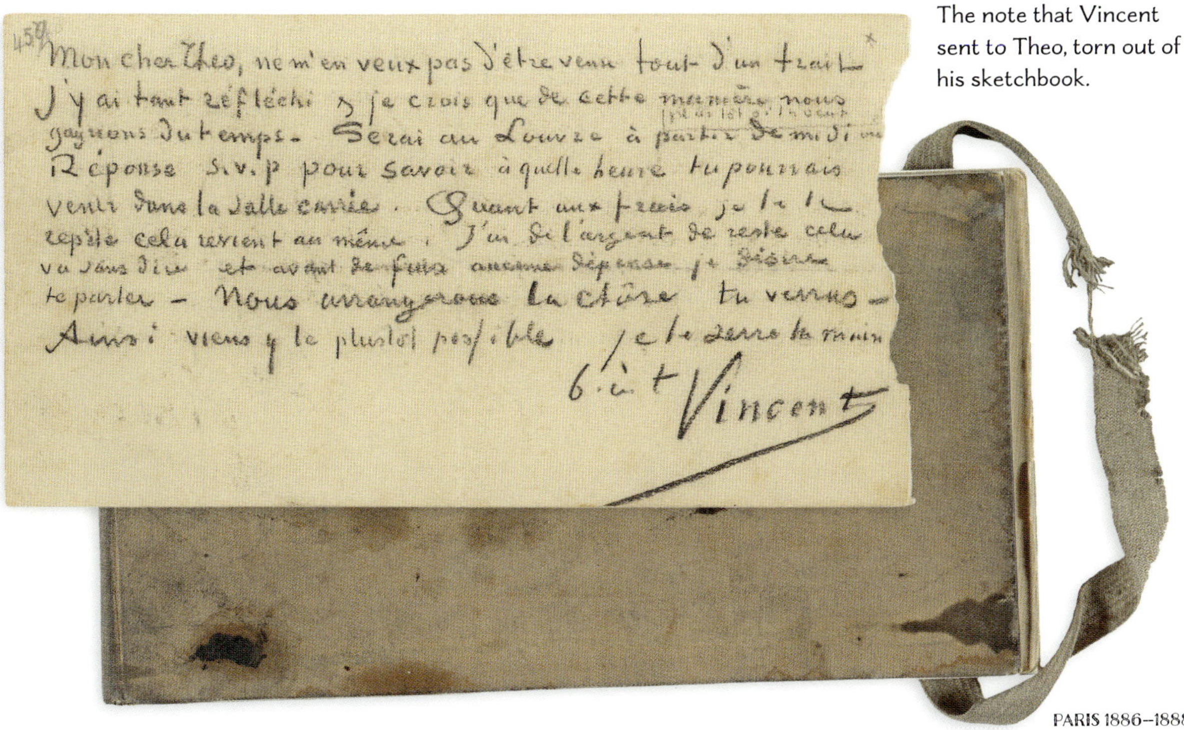
459

Mon cher Theo, ne m'en veux pas d'être venu tout d'un trait
J'y ai tant réfléchi & je crois que de cette manière nous
gagnons du temps. Serai au Louvre à partir de midi ou plus tôt si tu veux
Réponse s.v.p pour savoir à quelle heure tu pourrais
venir dans la salle carrée. Quant aux frais je te le
répète cela revient au même. J'ai de l'argent de reste cela
va sans dire et avant de faire aucune dépense je désire
te parler – Nous arrangerons la chose tu verras –
Ainsi viens y le plustôt possible je te serre la main
t. à t. Vincent

The note that Vincent sent to Theo, torn out of his sketchbook.

Boulevard de Clichy (1887), one of the main streets in Montmartre.

Salon Carré

Vegetable gardens on the hill of Montmartre.

Windmills and vegetable gardens on *La butte Montmartre*, the hill in Montmartre. Vincent made a **painting** of this scene in 1886.

Living with Theo

Vincent and Theo lived together in the neighbourhood of Montmartre. Vincent had lived there before. He hadn't taken the time to look around then, though, because he preferred to bury his nose in the Bible. But this time he went out to explore. Montmartre was on a hill on the outskirts of Paris. On one half of the hill, there were still plenty of vegetable gardens and windmills. But the city of Paris was getting bigger and bigger, and there were lots of houses and other buildings on the other half of the hill. Many artists lived in the area. There were paint shops and galleries. Montmartre was also packed with cafés and restaurants. That meant there were lots of interesting subjects to draw and paint.

THEO

Rue Lepic, the street where Vincent and Theo lived.

Number 54 is just around the corner.

The view from Theo's apartment. Vincent painted it in 1887.

Vincent and Theo's apartment was on the fourth floor. There was a big living room and a bedroom for Theo. The brothers didn't cook in the kitchen themselves. A housekeeper did the cooking for them every day. Vincent slept in a small space in the hallway. The best thing about the apartment was the view of Paris. Vincent painted it a few times. According to Theo, you could see as much sky from their flat as you could if you were standing on a dune by the sea.

From left to right: Paul Gauguin, Emile Bernard and Henri de Toulouse-Lautrec.

Painters listening to the great master Fernand Cormon.

Cormon's studio

Many artists from abroad wanted to work for a while at a famous painter's studio in Paris. Vincent was no exception. He chose the studio of Fernand Cormon. Artists went there every day to draw and paint. The great artist Cormon himself came by once a week. He gave them tips and suggestions. Vincent kept going for three or four months, which was quite a long time for him. But then he decided that he'd had enough. He thought he wasn't learning much. He preferred to work at Theo's. This really was the last time that he started a course of study. He wrote to a friend that his work went better when he was alone. 'It's probably my fault,' he said.

Vincent did find something very important at Cormon's studio, though: friends. He met the painters Emile Bernard and Henri de Toulouse-Lautrec there. The three men went out together to the cafés and restaurants of Montmartre, where they spent the whole evening talking about art. They drew and painted each other and exchanged their work. They had big plans for the future. Vincent was keen to work with his friends. Imagine if they had a place where they could paint together!

Vincent in a café in Paris, drawn by his friend Henri in 1887.

Vincent found something very important in Paris: friends. They met in the cafés and restaurants of Montmartre, and they talked all evening about art.

The self-portraits that Vincent made in Paris. Do you see that he was starting to use more and more colours?

Colour

In Paris, Vincent saw for the first time what the French painters were doing. They used very different colours from the ones he was accustomed to. He worked in the dark shades that Dutch artists preferred. But that all changed in Paris. Vincent started to use more and more colours. His work changed from dark to light. He began painting in sweeping lines and dots, with thick paint and thin paint. He had a special trick to avoid wasting expensive paint. He used balls of wool in different colours to see in advance if those shades went together well. Vincent also painted different subjects in Paris than he had in the Netherlands and Belgium. He no longer went in search of poor people to use as models. Instead, he made an entire series of paintings of colourful flowers. They were less expensive than models. But if he did want to paint a portrait, he had also found a solution: he bought a mirror and started painting himself. He made no fewer than **twenty-five self-portraits** in Paris. If you line them up next to one another, you can see how quickly his work changed.

Vase with Gladioli and Chinese Asters, 1886

Self-Portrait as a Painter, 1887–1888

The balls of wool that Vincent used to see if colours went together well.

Photographs

There are only a few photos of Vincent. **This** is the only picture of Vincent during his time as an artist. It was taken in Asnières, a village near Paris. Lots of people went there on Sundays to sit by the water of the River Seine. The man looking towards the camera is Vincent's friend Emile Bernard. Frustratingly, we can see Vincent's back, but not his face. Vincent didn't like photography, so he probably didn't want to be in the picture. He thought portrait photographs were like dead things and that painted portraits showed life. He said they came 'from deep in the soul of the painter'. In his opinion, that was something a machine couldn't do.

Emile later created a portrait of his friend in a different way than with a photo or a painting. He described him in words. Emile said that Vincent had short red hair, a goatee beard and a ragged moustache. He was not a large man, but he was stocky. He was constantly smoking his pipe and working on a painting or a drawing. He had a piercing gaze and was always thinking about something. He had interesting ideas and big dreams. When he talked, he waved his hands around. On the negative side, conversations with Vincent could quickly turn into arguments. He got annoyed when people didn't agree with him. That, too, was typical of Vincent, Emile wrote.

Emile Bernard and Vincent's back by the River Seine in Asnières.

Bridge over the Seine at Asnières, 1887

Some of the hundreds of Japanese prints that Vincent and Theo collected.

Japanese prints

In Vincent's day, a Japan craze swept through Europe. People wanted to have Japanese things in their homes. There were even special shops in Paris where you could buy vases, bowls, lanterns, fans and kimonos from Japan. Painters, including Vincent, collected Japanese prints. And of course, he pinned some of them to the walls of his room. Vincent and Theo had hundreds of these prints. He thought that the world looked very different in them. Simpler. With much more beautiful colours, lighter, and with clean lines. Vincent painted copies of the prints. He wanted to find out how the Japanese artists did it. For Vincent, Japan seemed like paradise. Painters worked there without arguing, out in the open air. He wanted to paint in that world, too.

Flowering Plum Orchard (after Hiroshige), 1887

In the Café: Agostina Segatori in Le Tambourin, 1887
Agostina is sitting at a tambourine-shaped table ('tambourin' in French), and the stools are also shaped like tambourines.

An exhibition

Vincent succeeded in having his work exhibited in Paris. The exhibition was at a café he often visited: Le Tambourin. He even started dating the owner of the café, Agostina Segatori. Vincent was really in love with her. You can see Agostina in the portrait he painted of her. She is sitting on a stool at a tambourine-shaped table. The stools are tambourines, too. If you look closely, you can see Japanese prints on the wall. Vincent was allowed to hang them there. He also exhibited a series of his own flower paintings at Le Tambourin. He hoped he would be able to sell them. Unfortunately, Agostina and Vincent fell out. Before Vincent could collect his paintings, the café was sold – with all the paintings in it.

Interior of a Restaurant, 1887
This is the restaurant in Paris where Vincent was allowed to display his work.

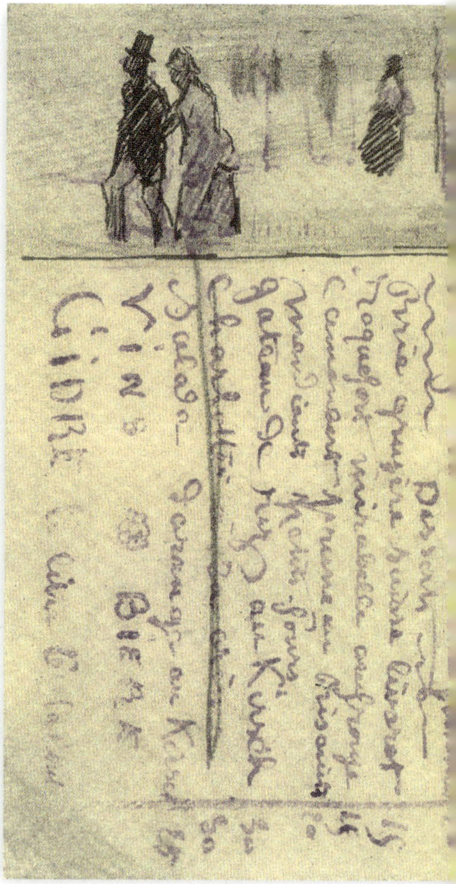

Sunflowers, 1887

Vincent also exhibited some paintings at the Grand Bouillon Restaurant du Chalet – work by himself and also by some other artists. Vincent was satisfied with this group exhibition. He didn't actually manage to sell any of his paintings, but the artist Paul Gauguin came to take a look. He had just returned from the island of Martinique in the Caribbean, where he had done a lot of painting. Paul invited Vincent to come and see his work. Vincent took Theo with him, who immediately bought a number of works to sell at the gallery. Vincent was very enthusiastic about Paul's work, too. He admired Paul, who had already travelled to paradise, while Vincent himself had only dreamed about it. They agreed to exchange paintings. Paul chose two of Vincent's flower paintings – of sunflowers.

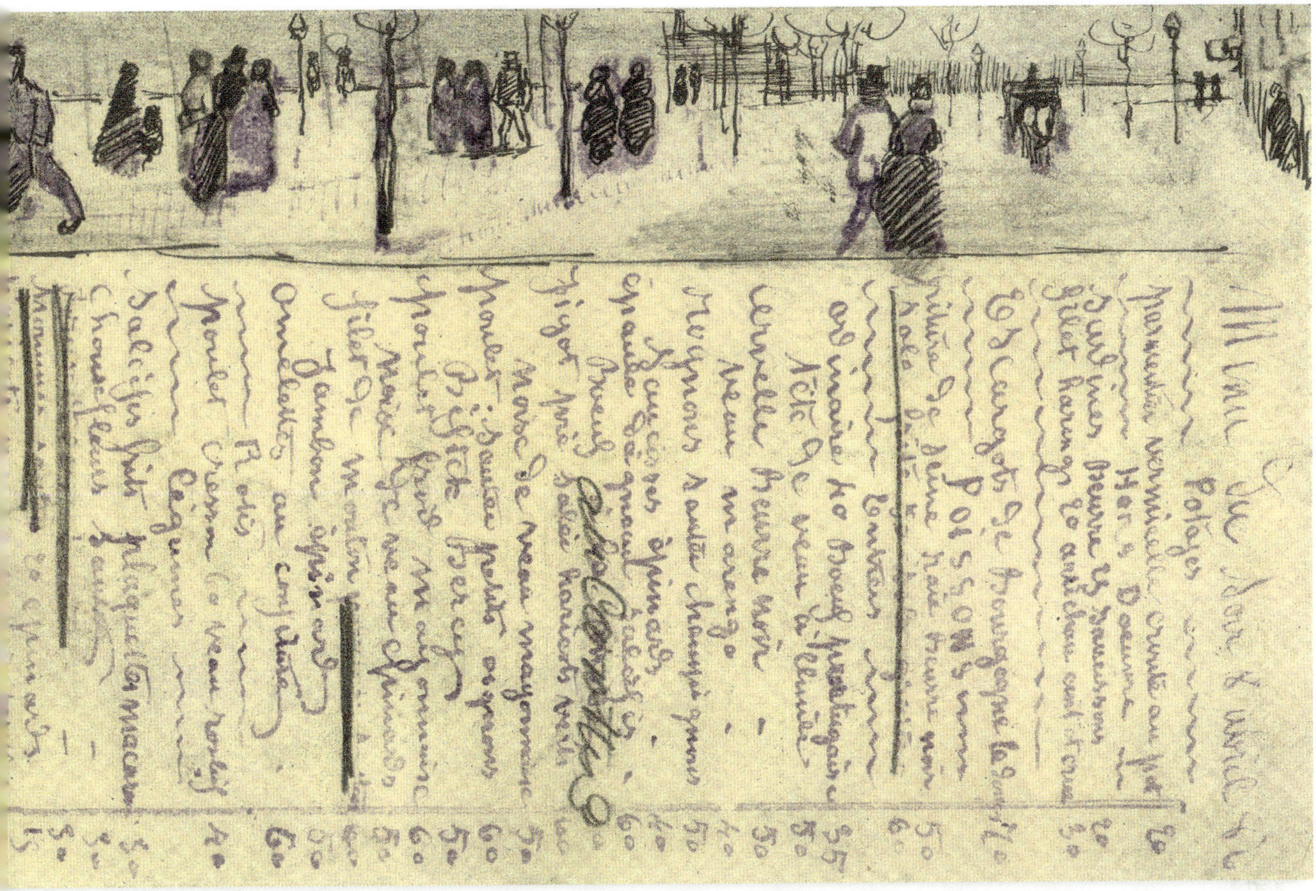

Sketches by Vincent on a menu, 1887.

Leaving Paris again

Living with Vincent wasn't always easy for Theo. Vincent got into fights with everyone. It reached a point where no one wanted to visit anymore, Theo complained in a letter to their sister Willemien. Sometimes he even went to live somewhere else for a while. Theo wrote that it was as if Vincent was two people. One day he was his beloved brother, who was so good at painting. Another day he was unkind and selfish. Then he seemed like a stranger. Living in Paris was becoming more and more difficult for Vincent, too. He disliked the busy city more and more. The galleries did not want to sell his work. The wine in the restaurants was disgusting, and the steak was fatty. Vincent longed for paradise: the Japan of the colourful prints. But it was a long way to Japan, so he chose the South of France instead. He had heard that the light and the colours there were better than in Paris. After two years with Theo, Vincent was moving on. He had made more than 200 paintings in Paris, and he left them with his brother. On a cold Sunday morning, Vincent boarded the train. He was going in search of Japan – but in France.

Vincent's best friend in Arles was Joseph Roulin. He lived near the Yellow House.
Joseph worked at the railway station in Arles, where the post trains arrived and departed.

ARLES
1888–1889

To the South of France

Vincent's journey to the south took a whole day and night. Can you imagine what it must have been like to bump about on a train with wooden benches for more than 700 kilometres? As he travelled, he thought about Theo. He was already missing him. But he was also fascinated by the view. All those colours! He saw big yellow rocks. Olive-green orchards. Grapevines in red soil, with lilac mountains in the background. Early in the morning, Vincent arrived in Arles, an old town with winding streets and ancient buildings.

A train at the station in Arles.

Bad weather

Vincent thought Arles was as beautiful as Japan. When he saw the South of France, he recognized the sky and the colours of his Japanese prints. It was exactly what he was looking for! He couldn't wait to get to work. But it was not very warm in the south. There was even a thick layer of snow. Working outside was impossible – it was far too cold. So, Vincent stayed in his hotel. He practised by painting a flowering twig of **an almond tree in a glass**. That allowed him to get down to work right away.

Sprig of Flowering Almond in a Glass, 1888

When the snow finally disappeared, the wind started to blow. It was the mistral, a strong and cold wind that sometimes lasts for days. That meant Vincent was still unable to work outside. His easel and canvases would have blown away. He went outside anyway, but only to go for walks and to look for subjects to paint. Fortunately, he found plenty of them.

Starry Night over the Rhône, 1888
The Rhône is the river that flows through Arles.

The Pink Orchard, 1888

Blossom

The fruit trees in the orchards in and around Arles were in bloom. Vincent found all those blossoming trees so beautiful that he refused to allow the mistral to hold him up any longer. He came up with a clever solution: he fixed his easel firmly into the ground with **iron pegs that were 50 centimetres long**.

Vincent couldn't get enough of the blossoming fruit trees. They reminded him of his Japanese prints, and they always remained one of his favourite subjects to paint. Flowering apricot, almond, apple, cherry, pear, peach and plum trees – Vincent painted them all. He set to work so frantically that he was afraid he would run out of paint.

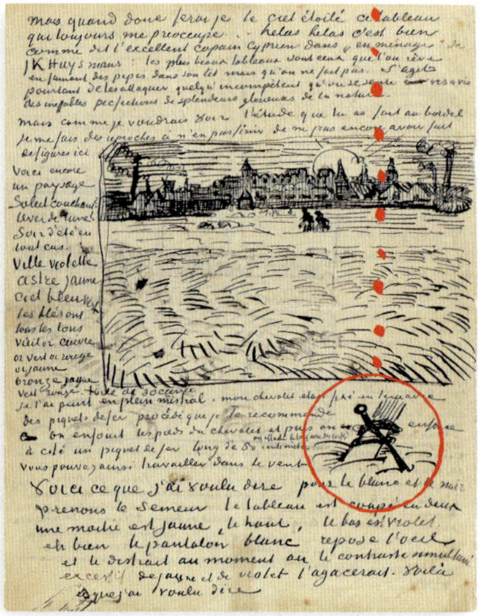

mais quand donc ferai je le ciel étoilé ce tableau
qui toujours me preoccupe. – helas helas c'est bien
comme dit l'excellent copain Cyprien dans "en ménage" de
JK Huysmans : les plus beaux tableaux sont ceux que l'on rêve
en fumant des pipes dans son lit mais qu'on ne fait pas.
pourtant de les attaquer quelqu'incompétent qu'on se sente
des ineffables perfections de splendeurs glorieuses de la nature.
mais comme je voudrais voir l'étude que tu as fait au bordel
je me fais des reproches à n'en plus finir de ne pas encore avoir fait
de figures ici

Voici encore
un paysage
Soleil couchant?
lever de lune?
Soir d'été en
tout cas.
Ville violette
astre jaune
ciel bleu vert
les blés ont
tous les tons
vieil or cuivre
or vert or rouge
or jaune
bronze jaune
vert rouge.

je l'ai peint en plein mistral. mon chevalet était fixé en terre
des piquets de fer procédé que je te recommande
on enfonce les pieds du chevalet et puis on enfonce
à côté un piquet de fer long de 50 centimètres
vous pouvez ainsi travailler dans le vent

Voici ce que j'ai voulu dire pour le blanc et le noir
prenons le Semeur le tableau est coupé en deux
une moitié est jaune, le haut, le bas est violet.
eh bien le pantalon blanc repose l'oeil
et le distrait au moment où le contraste simultané
excessif de jaune et de violet l'agacerait. voilà
ce que j'ai voulu dire

Letter (1888) from Vincent to his friend Emile Bernard.

The Pink Peach Tree, 1888

Bridge at Arles (Pont de Langlois), 1888

Drawbridge

Vincent kept finding new places to paint in Arles. Not far from his hotel, there was a canal that flowed all the way to the Mediterranean Sea. When a boat came to a bridge, the bridge sometimes had to be raised to let it pass through. **The French drawbridges** reminded Vincent of the Netherlands, where the bridges looked very similar. There were other things he recognized from home too. He wrote to Theo: 'Many of the subjects here are just the same as in Holland. **The difference is in the colour**.' For a painter who was in love with colour, Vincent believed the South of France was the place to be.

Field with Irises near Arles, 1888

Landscape with Windmills at Fontvieille, 1888

Did these windmills remind Vincent of the Netherlands?

The windmill 'De Gooyer' in Amsterdam, 1891.

White Cottages in Saintes-Maries, 1888

Vincent took three canvases and a supply of drawing paper to the sea with him. After he returned home, he also made some of the drawings into paintings.

The Mediterranean

When Vincent wanted to work outside, he had to take a lot of equipment with him: tubes of paint, brushes, an easel and large, unwieldy canvases that were sometimes empty and sometimes wet with paint. **This painting shows him walking on a very hot day**, with all his equipment. It's a self-portrait called *The Painter on the Road to Tarascon*. That was twenty kilometres away! When you look at the painting, you can almost feel the heat.

Vincent also wanted to visit the Mediterranean because he'd never seen it before. However, it was much too far for him to walk there with all his painting gear. He was going to stay for a few days in a fishing village, but there was no railway line to the place. He had to travel in a 'diligence' instead: **a stagecoach** pulled by horses. It was a bumpy five-hour ride from Arles to the sea, but the hard journey was worth the effort.

The Mediterranean Sea wasn't just blue. Vincent wrote to Theo that it had a shifting colour, like **the skin of a mackerel**. Green, purple, blue, pink or grey... Every second, there was a different colour. Vincent thought the sea and the village were beautiful subjects to paint. But he didn't know if he would be able to take his art with him when he returned home. He was afraid his wet paintings would be damaged by all the bumping around on the journey.

Tarascon Stagecoach, 1888

View of Saintes-Maries-de-la-Mer, 1888

Boats in Les Saintes-Maries-de-la-Mer, the fishing village where Vincent saw the Mediterranean.

There are grains of sand in the paint of *Seascape near Les Saintes-Maries-de-la-Mer* (1888). Perhaps the wind was blowing when Vincent was painting. Or maybe he'd dropped his brush on the beach.

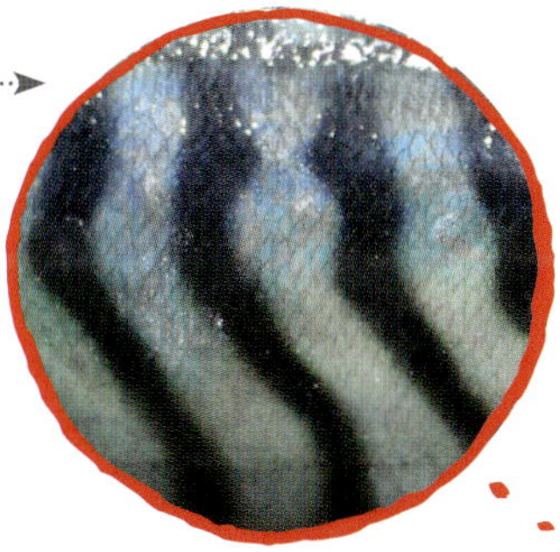

The Yellow House (The Street), 1888

An angry hotel owner

Vincent worked very hard, drawing and painting whatever he could. If you make lots of paintings, you also need a lot of space. That's because the paint has to dry, which can take days. So, you can't just stack up all your new paintings. When Vincent's room was full, he put the wet paintings in the corridor and in various places around the hotel. The hotel owner wasn't at all happy about that. They ended up having an argument. Vincent thought the man was just a moaner. The room was quite expensive, and the hotel food wasn't good. Vincent thought the wine tasted like 'poison'. He wanted a place of his own in Arles. He found a small, Yellow House on a square with beautiful gardens. When the sun shone, there was light throughout the house. In the Yellow House, Vincent could leave his paintings wherever he liked, without anyone complaining about it.

The Yellow House in a photograph from the early 20th century.

Path in the Park, 1888

The Park and Pond in Front of the Yellow House, 1888

Studio of the South

In Paris, Vincent had dreamed of having a place where he could live and work with friends and where they could learn from one another. He wanted the Yellow House to become such a place, a 'Studio of the South'. Vincent invited all his friends to come to Arles. He selected the furniture with great care. He bought beds, chairs, tables and other bits and pieces for the house. He made the nicest room into a guestroom, perhaps for Paul Gauguin, who had said he would come to join him. Vincent wanted it to look elegant, with white walls and paintings of sunflowers in a vase. Vincent remembered from Paris that Paul loved sunflowers. And he hoped his brother would often come to visit too. How could Theo stand living in the busy city of Paris?

Sunflowers, 1888

New friends

Vincent's own bedroom in the Yellow House was very simple, with plain wooden furniture. He was so pleased with the room that he made three paintings of it. He sent one of them to his mother and sister in the Netherlands. There were paintings in the bedroom too: portraits of new friends from Arles. On the right, you can see Eugène Boch, who lived in a village outside Arles. Eugène was an artist who 'dreams great dreams', Vincent wrote to Theo. Vincent thought his new friend looked like a poet. So, he called the painting *The Poet*, even though Eugène didn't write poetry. The painting of another new friend hung next to it. That friend was in the French army, and his name was Paul-Eugène Milliet. He often accompanied Vincent on his long walks. They talked about books and art, and Vincent gave his friend drawing lessons. A lot of girls in Arles thought Paul-Eugène was a handsome man. Vincent was secretly a bit jealous. He named the portrait of his friend *The Lover.*

In Arles, Vincent and Eugène liked to visit a café with a large terrace, and Vincent later painted it. As a result, the café is now famous.

EUGÈNE

PAUL-EUGÈNE

The 'postman' and his family

Vincent's best friend in Arles, though, was **Joseph Roulin**. Joseph lived near the Yellow House and worked at the railway station in Arles. Post trains arrived and departed there, transporting hundreds of letters, postcards and parcels every day. Joseph was responsible for making sure that everything ran smoothly. When they became friends, Vincent gained a lot of new models. He was allowed to paint everyone in Joseph's family. They felt very honoured! He painted Joseph himself, in his blue uniform with gold trim, and also **his wife** and their children: **baby Marcelle** and the brothers **Armand** and **Camille**. The whole family is famous now – because they were painted by Vincent.

JOSEPH ROULIN

BABY MARCELLE

MRS ROULIN

CAMILLE

ARMAND

The ruin that Vincent often walked to.

Landscape

In the summer, the farmers of Arles had to work hard. It was time for the harvest: reaping the wheat, picking the fruit and vegetables. Like the farmers, Vincent spent all day in the fields. He drew and painted farms with big stacks of hay in the yard and landscapes with green and yellow fields as far as the eye could see. Do you see **the tower on the left in the distance**, in his painting *The Harvest*? It's an old ruin, which Vincent walked to often, about fifty times in fact, ten kilometres there and back. The heat, the colours, the chirping of the **cicadas**... For Vincent, the French landscape seemed like a world that would always exist. A world without an end. And in his painted landscapes, that's true: time stands still forever.

The Harvest, 1888

A cicada is an insect that feeds on the sap of plants. Cicadas make a lot of noise, and you can often hear them in southern Europe. Vincent drew this cicada in a letter to Theo.

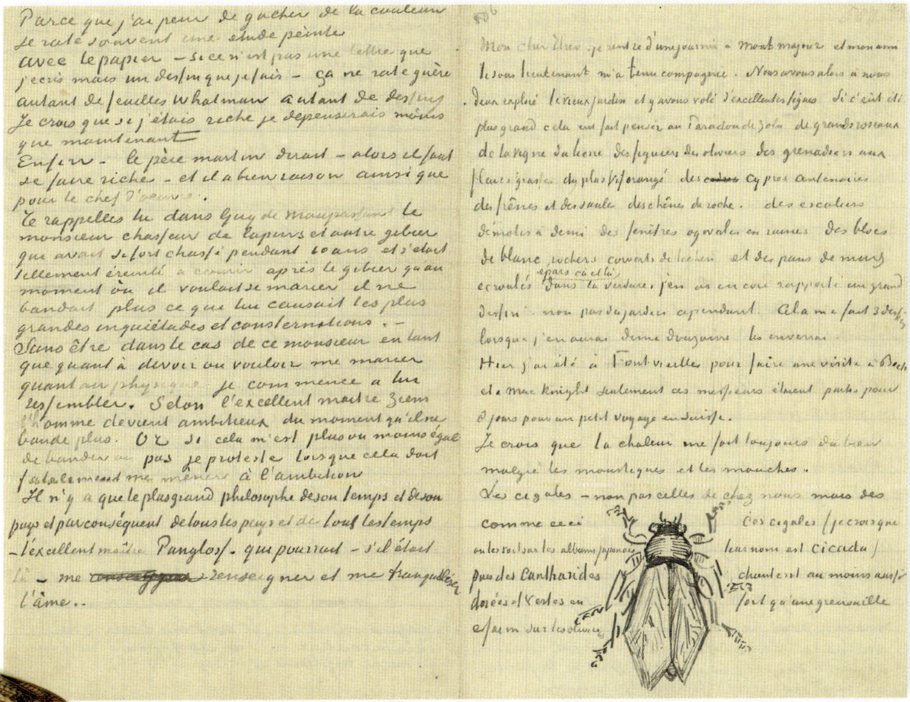

Parce que j'ai peur de gâcher de la couleur
je rate souvent une étude peinte
avec le papier – si ce n'est pas une lettre que
j'écris mais un dessin que je fais – ça ne rate guère
autant de feuilles Whatman autant de dessins
Je crois que si j'étais riche je dépenserais moins
que maintenant
Enfin – le père Martin dirait – alors il faut
se faire riche – et il a bien raison ainsi que
pour le chef d'oeuvre.
Te rappelles tu dans Guy de Maupassant le
monsieur chasseur de lapins et autre gibier
qui avait si fort chassé pendant 10 ans et s'était
tellement éreinté à courir après le gibier qu'au
moment où il voulait se marier il ne
bandait plus ce qui lui causait les plus
grandes inquiétudes et consternations. –
Sans être dans le cas de ce monsieur en tant
que quant à devoir ou vouloir me marier
quant au physique je commence à lui
ressembler. Selon l'excellent maître Ziem
l'homme devient ambitieux du moment qu'il ne
bande plus. Or si cela m'est plus ou moins égal
de bander ou pas je proteste lorsque cela doit
fatalement me mener à l'ambition
Il n'y a que le plus grand philosophe de son temps et de son
pays et par conséquent de tous les pays et de tous les temps
– l'excellent maître Pangloss – qui pourrait – s'il était
là – me ~~conseiller~~ renseigner et me tranquilliser
l'âme..

Mon cher Theo, je rentre d'une journée à Montmajour et mon ami
le sous lieutenant m'a tenu compagnie. Nous avons alors à nous
deux exploré le vieux jardin et y avons volé d'excellentes figues. Si c'eût été
plus grand cela eût fait penser au Paradou de Zola. de grands roseaux
de la vigne du lierre des figuiers des oliviers des grenadiers aux
fleurs grasses du plus vif orangé des ~~cedres~~ cyprès centenaires
des frênes et des saules des chênes de roche. des escaliers
démolis à demi des fenêtres ogivales en ruines des blocs
de blanc rochers couverts de lichen et des pans de murs
écroulés épars çà et là dans la verdure, j'en ai encore rapporté un grand
dessin. non pas du jardin cependant. Cela me fait 3 dessins
lorsque j'en aurai demi douzaine les enverrai.
Hier j'ai été à Fontvieille pour faire une visite à Boch
et à Mac Knight seulement ces messieurs étaient partis pour
8 jours pour un petit voyage en Suisse.
Je crois que la chaleur me fait toujours du bien
malgré les moustiques et les mouches.
Les cigales – non pas celles de chez nous mais des
comme ceci
on les voit sur les albums japonais
pas des Cantharides
dorées et vertes en
essaim sur les oliviers
Ces cigales (je crois que
leur nom est cicada)
chantent au moins aussi
fort qu'une grenouille

The artists' house

In real life, of course, time ticked on. 'I'm working like a painting-locomotive,' Vincent wrote to Theo. In Arles, he made around 180 paintings. Then he received a letter from Paul Gauguin, who told Vincent that he was coming to Arles. 'That will make a big change in your life,' wrote Theo, who hoped that his brother's dream would come true and that Vincent's house would become a place where other artists would also feel at home. Then Vincent would no longer be alone.

Vincent started working even harder, to make sure that the Yellow House would be ready and that Paul's bedroom would be decorated with paintings of sunflowers in time. He sometimes worked for twelve hours in a row – and even through the night. As a result, when Paul arrived, Vincent was ill. You must have been working too hard again and not taking care of yourself, Theo said. He was right, though: after Paul arrived, Vincent's life changed.

Paul Gauguin's *Self-Portrait with Portrait of Emile Bernard (Les misérables)*, 1888

Arguments

Paul didn't actually want to go and live with Vincent. He did it for Theo, who sold his paintings in Paris. Paul often ran out of money, so he wanted to stay friends with Vincent's brother. That was why he went to Arles.

At first, sharing the house worked out quite well. Vincent and Paul went out together to paint. They talked about art. They did the housework together. Vincent thought Paul was a very good cook. But before long they started to disagree, about the best subjects to paint, for example, and about how messy Paul thought Vincent was. There were brushes and tubes of paint everywhere. And Vincent spent far too much money. Their good conversations turned into discussions. Their discussions turned into arguments. Vincent wrote to Theo: 'We sometimes emerge from it with tired minds, like an electric battery after it's run down.' And Paul wrote to Theo that he wanted to return to Paris: 'Vincent and I absolutely cannot live together without problems.' They were too different. That's what happens sometimes. You want to be friends, but it doesn't work out.

The ear

Everything turned out differently than Vincent had hoped. Hard work and disagreements were not a good combination. Vincent's body was tired, and so was his mind. Paul was making plans to leave. And then everything went wrong. Really wrong. We don't know exactly what happened, but just before Christmas Vincent collapsed. He and Paul probably had a big fight. Paul said later that Vincent had threatened him with a razor. But is that really true? Whatever the case, Vincent became very confused. So confused that he did something terrible: he cut off his own left ear.

Self Portrait with Bandaged Ear, 1889

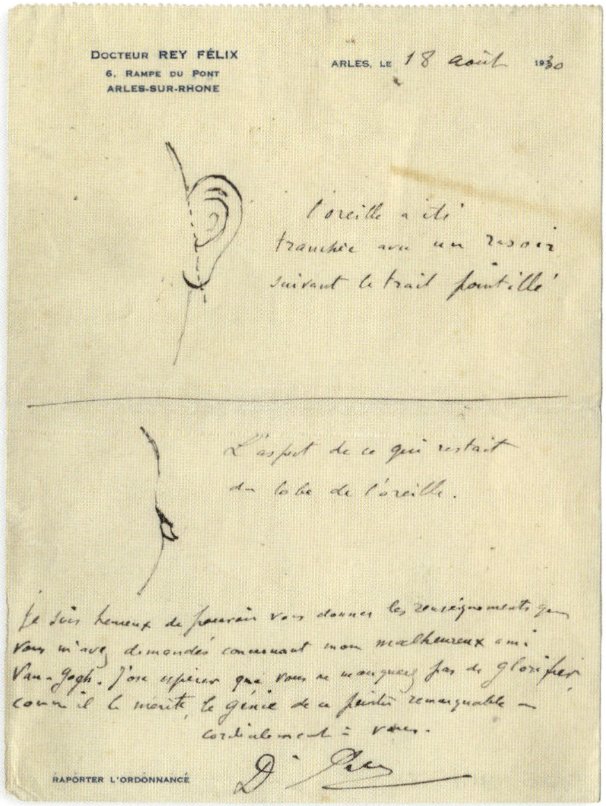

Docteur REY FÉLIX
6, Rampe du Pont
Arles-sur-Rhone

Arles, le 18 août 1930

l'oreille a été tranchée avec un rasoir suivant le trait pointillé

L'aspect de ce qui restait du lobe de l'oreille.

Je suis heureux de pouvoir vous donner les renseignements que vous m'avez demandés concernant mon malheureux ami Van-Gogh. J'ose espérer que vous ne manquerez pas de glorifier comme il le mérite, le génie de ce peintre remarquable —
Cordialement à vous.
Dr Rey

RAPPORTER L'ORDONNANCE

Forty-two years later, Vincent's doctor made a sketch of what was left of Vincent's ear.

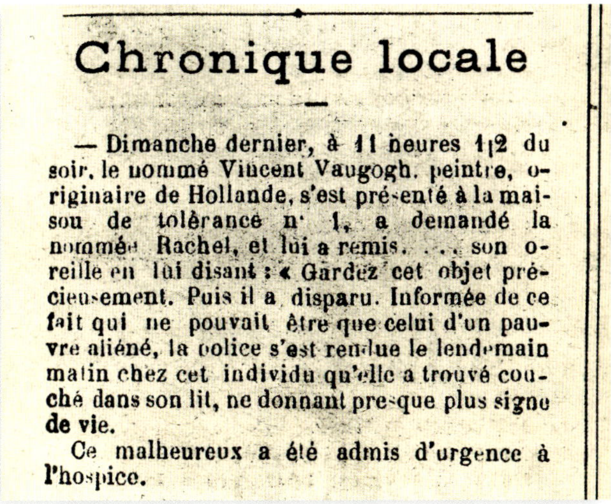

Chronique locale

— Dimanche dernier, à 11 heures 1/2 du soir, le nommé Vincent Vaugogh, peintre, originaire de Hollande, s'est présenté à la maison de tolérance n° 1, a demandé la nommée Rachel, et lui a remis.... son oreille en lui disant : « Gardez cet objet précieusement. Puis il a disparu. Informée de ce fait qui ne pouvait être que celui d'un pauvre aliéné, la police s'est rendue le lendemain matin chez cet individu qu'elle a trouvé couché dans son lit, ne donnant presque plus signe de vie.

Ce malheureux a été admis d'urgence à l'hospice.

'Last Sunday evening, at half past eleven, Vincent van Gogh, a painter from Holland, presented himself at...' This is the beginning of a French newspaper article from 1888. It reports what happened after Vincent cut off his ear. He gave it to someone and then he disappeared. The police found him a day later – at home in his Yellow House, in bed. Vincent had lost a lot of blood and was rushed to hospital.

The hospital in Arles

Paul sent a message to Theo in Paris, who immediately took the night train to Arles. On Christmas morning, he sat beside Theo's bed in the hospital. It was a flying visit because Theo didn't actually have any time. He had something else on his mind: he'd fallen in love with Jo Bonger, a girl from Amsterdam. Theo had asked her to marry him. She'd turned him down at first, but now she had said yes. They were going to celebrate their engagement in the Netherlands in January.

Vincent's doctor told Theo that Vincent was suffering from nervous exhaustion. He thought it would pass. Vincent's wounded ear was patched up nicely. That reassured Theo a little. He caught the train straight back to Paris, 750 kilometres away. Paul went with him. Vincent would never see his friend again. Luckily, he had other friends, like Joseph, who came to fetch him when he was allowed to go home two weeks later. Joseph wrote to tell Theo that Vincent was doing well: 'He is as meek as a lamb.' In good spirits, Vincent returned to the Yellow House. But sadly, things did not go as well as he had hoped. At the beginning of February, Vincent collapsed for the second time. He had to go back to hospital. After some weeks, he was allowed to return home, but he soon had another attack.

The Ward in the Hospital at Arles, 1889

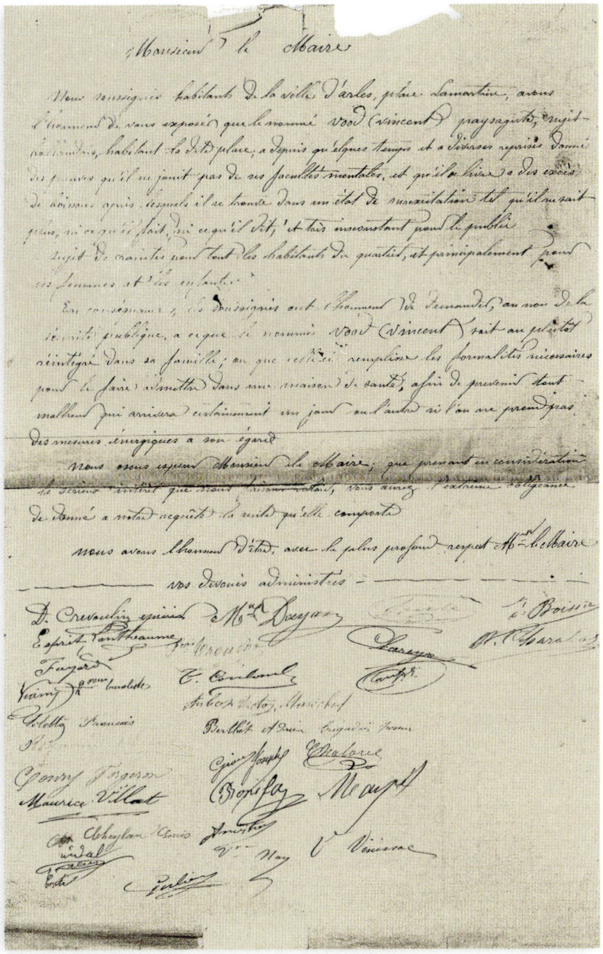

Monsieur le Maire

Nous soussignés habitants de la ville d'arles, place Lamartine, avons l'honneur de vous exposer que le nommé Vood (Vincent) paysagiste, sujet hollandais, habitant la dite place, a depuis quelques temps et à diverses reprises donné des preuves qu'il ne jouit pas de ses facultés mentales, et qu'il se livre à des excès de boissons après lesquels il se trouve dans un état de surexcitation tel qu'il ne sait plus, ni ce qu'il fait, ni ce qu'il dit, et très inconstant pour le public sujet de craintes pour tous les habitants du quartier, et principalement pour les femmes et les enfants.

En conséquence, les soussignés ont l'honneur de demander, au nom de la sécurité publique, à ce que le nommé Vood (Vincent) soit au plutôt réintégré dans sa famille, ou que celle-ci remplisse les formalités nécessaires pour le faire admettre dans une maison de santé, afin de prévenir tout malheur qui arrivera certainement un jour ou l'autre si l'on ne prend pas des mesures énergiques à son égard.

Nous osons espérer Monsieur le Maire, que prenant en considération le sérieux intérêt que nous faisons valoir, vous aurez l'extrême obligeance de donner à notre requête la suite qu'elle comporte.

Nous avons l'honneur d'être, avec le plus profond respect Mr le Maire

vos dévoués administrés

D. Crevoulin épicier

Esprit Pantheaume

Fayard

Maurice Villat

Locked up

The people who lived near the Yellow House thought Vincent was dangerous. They called him the 'fou roux' – the 'red-headed madman'. They said Vincent drank too much alcohol and behaved strangely. Some of them thought he should leave. They wrote **a letter to the mayor**. After a police investigation, Vincent was admitted to a hospital in Arles, against his will. But his condition didn't improve much. He saw things that weren't there and was even locked up on his own in a room for a while, so that he could cool down. He was in a very gloomy frame of mind. Theo was obviously upset that Vincent was so unwell, while he himself was so happy with Jo. They were going to get married and had found a home in Paris. It was already full of Vincent's paintings. He wrote to Vincent that it was 'So cheerful!' But Theo didn't have time to come to Arles again.

The Courtyard of the Hospital at Arles, 1889

Leaving Arles

Vincent's doctors thought that he shouldn't return home. Now and then he was allowed to go outside, but not on his own. Carefully, he started to do a little painting again. Vincent didn't have many friends left in Arles. His good friend Joseph had a new job in a different town. Eugène had returned to Belgium, and Paul-Eugène had left to work in Africa. Vincent discussed the situation with Theo. He decided that he wanted to go to a hospital for people with mental health problems. An 'asylum' where the 'insane' were treated – that was how they described it in Vincent's day.

'In all I've had 4 big crises in which I hadn't the slightest idea of what I said, wanted, did,' Vincent wrote to his sister Willemien. He was afraid of going to the hospital, but he was even more afraid that the attacks would return. But he kept his spirits up: 'I hope there will come a time when I paint again, even if it is in the asylum.'

Two Poplars in the Alpilles near Saint-Rémy, 1889

SAINT-RÉMY

1889–1890

Postcard of Saint-Rémy.

The patients' names were written in a book. You can see Vincent's name here.

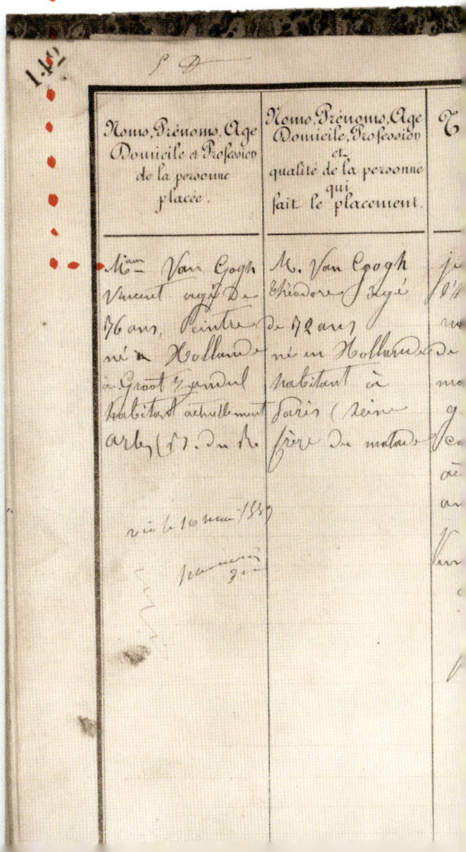

The hospital in Saint-Rémy

The hospital that Vincent went to was near the town of Saint-Rémy, twenty-five kilometres from Arles. Vincent travelled there by train, and someone went with him, in case he had an attack during the journey. The doctor at the hospital in Saint-Rémy told Vincent he was suffering from a form of epilepsy. That meant he wasn't 'mad', but sick. What a relief! But it was hard to predict when he would have one of his attacks, as there was always a long interval between them. Vincent had to be admitted for 'long-term observation' – his doctor wanted to keep a close eye on him for a while.

Vincent wrote that the hospital was like a kind of zoo. There was a lot of screaming and shouting. But it wasn't as bad as he had imagined. The patients were well cared for, and they were nice to each other. Vincent was happy to be there, even on the first day. He'd never felt so calm. Calm enough to start painting again soon, he wrote to Theo and Jo, his new wife. Now that Theo was married, he might have children before long. Vincent thought it was about time for him to start earning his own money – and soon.

At first Vincent wasn't allowed to leave the hospital, but he could still paint in the garden there.
He started with two paintings of flowers: irises and lilacs. The other patients came to see what he was doing.

The hospital in Saint-Rémy
A. Vincent's room
B. Vincent's studio

Vincent's room

Vincent was given a small room on the first floor. There were iron bars on the windows, but the view was wonderful. In the morning, the sun rose over green fields. Far in the distance, he saw the Alpilles, a small range of mountains. Sometimes they were grey. Sometimes they were blue. Such beautiful colours! Even in and around the hospital, Vincent found plenty of subjects to paint. Lots of the rooms were empty, so Vincent was given an extra one, which he used as a studio.

Window in the Studio, 1889

Vincent painted the mountain landscape from his window: *Enclosed Wheatfield with Rising Sun*, 1889

Did Vincent really have epilepsy?

That's a good question. Lots and lots of doctors have thought about this over the years. Doctors nowadays know more than doctors did in Vincent's day. It's possible that he was suffering from an illness that was unknown at the time. The problem is that there's no way for doctors now to examine Vincent. All they can do is study what the doctors said about him at the time, and what Vincent and his family wrote about it. And everyone reads that information in their own way, of course. The more modern doctors have suggested all kinds of different illnesses. Some of them have even thought that Vincent was poisoned by the oil paint he used. Others have blamed the gas lighting in the Yellow House. But the only correct answer we can give to that question is: we simply don't know.

1

The window of t he room where Vincent had his studio. This photograph was taken in the 1950s.

Vincent's room, photograph from the 1950s.

2

Garden of the Asylum, 1889
In the background, Vincent painted part of the wall around the hospital grounds.

Lilac Bush, 1889

Irises, 1889

The garden

At first, Vincent wasn't allowed to leave the hospital, but he could paint in the garden. He started with two pictures of flowers: irises and lilacs. The other patients came to see what he was doing. Vincent wrote that they were modest and polite, and they left him alone. It was nice that the patients were allowed to go outdoors, but they weren't completely free, of course. In some of Vincent's paintings, you can see why: there was **a high wall around the garden** to make sure that the patients were unable to leave without permission.

Another attack

For a month or two, everything went quite well for Vincent. He was given permission to paint outside the hospital grounds, as long as there was someone to accompany him. Vincent headed into the mountains with his painting equipment. While he was working, he suddenly had a heavy feeling, a huge sense of loneliness. He felt that something was about to happen, that he was going to have an attack. But **he still finished his painting**. Back at the hospital, he became completely confused. This confusion went on for days. Vincent ate dirt off the floor. He drank paraffin, the fuel used for lamps. He ate oil paint and drank turpentine, too. Then he became very miserable. He didn't leave his room for a month. When he was allowed to paint again, he stayed inside and copied pictures of paintings by other artists. It was another month before he dared to venture back outside.

It is 'TERRIBLE,' Vincent wrote to Theo after his attack. It was clear that he was not getting any better and that the attacks would keep returning. And they did indeed – he had a few more attacks while he was in hospital. However, each time, he recovered and continued to draw and paint. In his year in Saint-Rémy, Vincent made 150 paintings and 150 drawings.

Entrance to a Quarry, 1890

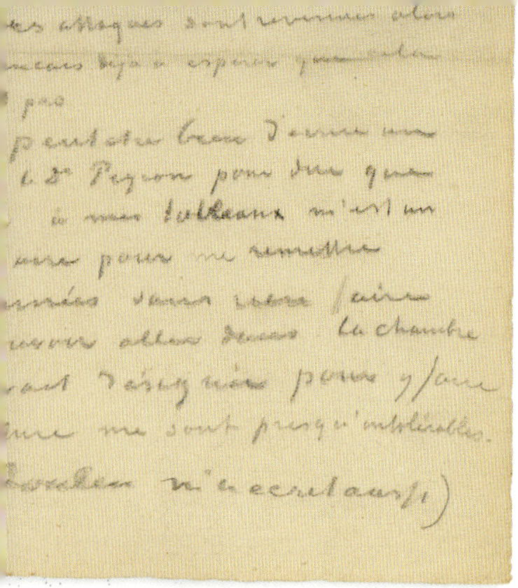
...es attaques sont revenues alors
...cas il y a espoir que cela
pas
peut être bien d'écrire un
à Dr Peyron pour dire que
à mes tableaux m'est un
...pour me remettre
...années sans rien faire
avoir aller dans la chambre
...t désigné pour y/aux
...me sont presqu'intolérables.
...n'ai écrit aussi)

After his attack, Vincent wrote a letter to Theo. He was not allowed to use an ink pen, as the nurses were afraid he would use it to hurt himself. So, he wrote with crayon instead.

Hydrotherapy

'Now I take a bath twice a week, and stay in it for two hours,' Vincent wrote to Theo. This bathing was part of his treatment. It was officially called 'hydrotherapy'. 'Hydro' means 'water'. The hospital used a system of 'contrast bathing', which involved first sitting in warm water and then in cold water or having a cold shower after a nice hot bath. The doctors said it had a calming effect. It seemed to work on Vincent. But it didn't work for everyone. When one new patient arrived, Vincent wrote: 'up to now he's scarcely calmed down, although he's in a bath all day long.'

Vincent wants to leave

Eventually, Vincent had had enough. He was very bored and he wanted to leave the hospital. He wrote to Theo that the thought of living any longer with 'the mad people here' upset him. How could he be expected to work? He wanted to return to the north, to live closer to Theo and Jo. They now had a son, who was called Vincent Willem, after his uncle. Vincent was touched that they'd named their son after him. As a gift, he painted *Almond Blossom*: branches of flowering almond trees, which he could see from his hospital room. Theo and Jo hung the painting above their piano.

Almond Blossom, 1890

Recognition and compliments

Life was not easy for Vincent. He worked so hard and there were so few people who appreciated his work. But that was slowly changing. More and more people were starting to find Vincent's work beautiful and interesting. Theo also thought the work that Vincent had made in Arles was 'superb'. He sent six of Vincent's paintings to an exhibition in Brussels, Belgium. Albert Aurier, an important art expert, wrote compliments about Vincent in a magazine. Paul Gauguin sent an enthusiastic letter about the exhibition. He wanted to exchange another painting with Vincent. And one of Vincent's paintings was actually sold: ***The Red Vineyard*** (1888). The buyer was Anna Boch, the sister of Vincent's friend Eugène. Sadly, though, Vincent no longer believed in his own success. He didn't think he deserved all those compliments. He wanted Mr Aurier to stop writing so enthusiastically about his paintings. It made him nervous.

View of the Alpilles, 1890

Leaving Saint-Rémy

In the meantime, Theo had found a new place for Vincent: Auvers-sur-Oise, a village near Paris. Other artists worked there too, and there was a doctor who could look after Vincent. That was important in case he had an attack. Vincent didn't want to be immediately admitted to hospital again. In May 1890, he left the hospital and moved to Auvers. But first he went to stay in Paris. Vincent wanted to meet Theo's wife Jo and their son. He couldn't wait to see his brother again. It had been more than a year! Vincent couldn't remember much about Theo's visit to the hospital in Arles. Theo was worried about Vincent's long train journey. What if his brother had an attack? But Vincent insisted on travelling alone. He just needed to stay calm.

When a crowing rooster startled little Vincent Willem, Uncle Vincent laughed.
'And the cockerel goes cocorico!' he said. That's French for 'cock-a-doodle-doo'.

Farmhouse, 1890

Houses at Auvers, 1890

AUVERS-SUR-OISE

1890

Visiting Paris

Luckily, Vincent's journey went well. Carrying his belongings, he got off the train in Paris the next morning. Theo came to meet him at the station. They went home in a horse-drawn cab. **Theo's wife Jo** was keeping a lookout for them. Vincent looked very different from what she had imagined. He did not appear to be sick, but was 'a sturdy man, with broad shoulders and a healthy colour,' as she later wrote. Jo even thought that Vincent looked cheerful. Vincent felt emotional when he met his young nephew, who was also called Vincent. And he was, of course, reunited with a lot of his paintings, which were now hanging on Theo and Jo's walls. Vincent wanted to stay in Paris for fourteen days. But after only three days, he'd had enough of the noise and the bustle of the big city. He wasn't used to it any more. He caught a train and travelled to Auvers-sur-Oise, thirty kilometres away.

The countryside of Auvers, with the railway line in the background: *Landscape with Carriage and Train*, 1890

Arrival in Auvers

The first thing Vincent wrote to Theo and Jo was how beautiful he thought Auvers was. The village was on a hill, with big fields all around, where crops of grain, potatoes and beans grew. Vincent thought that Theo and Jo should come and join him in Auvers. It was much healthier than living in the city. As he always did, Vincent went for long walks in his new surroundings, looking for subjects for his work. He was particularly keen to paint the **old-fashioned houses with their thatched roofs**. If he could sell his paintings, he would be able to cover his expenses in Auvers. Then he wouldn't need Theo's money anymore. To save money, Vincent didn't rent a whole house as he had done in Arles. He found a cheap room at the Auberge Ravoux, an inn close to the station and the town hall.

The Church at Auvers, 1890

The Oise at Auvers, 1890

Vincent's new home was by the River Oise. You can see it in the background.

This is the inn where Vincent rented a room. The girl in the doorway is the owner's daughter. Vincent painted a portrait of her.

The Town Hall at Auvers, 1890
The flags in this painting are for the French national holiday on 14 July. Did you notice that this building looks like the town hall in Zundert? (See pp. 10–11.)

Portrait of Adeline Ravoux, 1890

Marguerite Gachet in the Garden, 1890

Dr Gachet's house

Vincent met Dr Paul Gachet in Auvers-sur-Oise. **Dr Gachet** lived in a large house, with his daughter Marguerite and his son Paul Junior. Dr Gachet was an amateur artist: he drew and painted in his spare time. The doctor collected paintings and knew a lot of famous artists. He'd agreed with Theo that he would keep an eye on Vincent. Vincent thought they would quickly become friends – and they did.

Dr Gachet lived in a house that was like an antiques shop. It was packed with old, dark objects. Vincent thought it was awful, but he still liked to visit. He was invited to dinner there a couple of times a week. In the beginning Vincent thought Dr Gachet was a bit of a strange man, but he immediately started work on a portrait of his new friend.

In Dr Gachet's opinion, Vincent was doing well. He was almost certain his attacks wouldn't return. The doctor thought Vincent just needed to work hard. That would help to lift his gloomy moods. So, Vincent worked hard. In the 70 days he lived in Auvers, he made more than 70 paintings and 150 drawings.

Portrait of Dr Gachet, 1890

Daubigny's garden

Vincent was allowed to paint in the garden of a famous artist in Auvers. It was a wonderful opportunity. But he didn't have a canvas to paint on! Luckily, he soon came up with a clever solution. He stretched a linen tea towel over a wooden frame, which meant he could get down to work. On the back of his painting ***Daubigny's Garden***, you can still see the red stripes of the tea towel.

Cock-a-doodle-doo

One big advantage of Auvers was that Paris was so close. You could easily travel there and back on the train in a day. When Theo and Jo came to visit Vincent, the doctor asked them to come for lunch in the garden, because it was a lovely day. Vincent went to meet them at the station. He had brought a bird's nest for his nephew to play with, and he showed him all the animals in the doctor's garden. There were quite a few! Vincent said that Dr Gachet had 'eight cats, three dogs, chickens, rabbits, ducks, pigeons...' When a crowing rooster startled little Vincent Willem, Uncle Vincent laughed. 'And the cockerel goes cocorico!' he said. That's French for 'cock-a-doodle-doo'.

Vincent always carried a sketchbook with him. When he saw something interesting, he would quickly draw it in his sketchbook. This sketchbook is Vincent's last one. He had it in Auvers, and he drew a dog, chickens and other subjects in it.

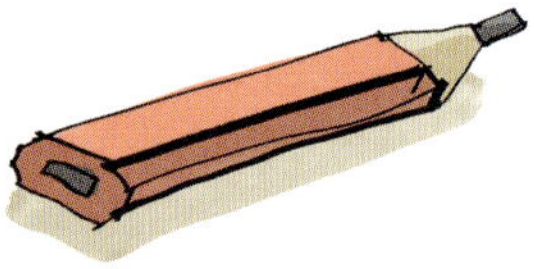

Visiting Paris

A few weeks later, Vincent went to Paris to visit Theo and Jo. But it wasn't much fun this time. There was trouble. Little Vincent Willem was ill, Jo was tired, and Theo was having problems at work. He wanted to leave his job and start his own art dealership. But that was not so simple. Theo had to earn money not only for his own family, but also for Vincent and for their mother. There was a lot of discussion – and it all became too much for Vincent. He travelled back to Auvers with a head full of worries. He had made hundreds of paintings but had still sold almost nothing. He was unable to take care of himself. Was he a burden on Theo and his family? Could Theo continue to support him financially if he resigned from his job? Vincent wrote a long and sad letter to Theo and Jo. Fortunately, they quickly replied to say there was no need for Vincent to worry.

Tree roots

If you needed wood for your stove in Auvers, you didn't have to look far. 'Coppice' trees grew on the slopes. You can see some on the postcard below. It was easy to chop off their branches, and new ones simply grew back on the stumps that were left. Within a couple of years, they were big enough to use again. The trees were a strange shape because of all that chopping and sawing, and Vincent thought they were interesting to paint. For his painting *Tree Roots,* he looked up at an angle. He could just make out a triangle of blue sky through the twisted trees.

Postcard that coincidentally shows the spot where Vincent painted *Tree Roots.* Do you recognize the shapes in the photograph?

Tree Roots, 1890

Wheatfield with Crows, 1890

The fields of Auvers

Vincent started working hard again. In the fields around Auvers, he painted three large landscapes of wheatfields under stormy skies. He wanted these paintings to demonstrate to Theo and Jo how much healthier life was in the countryside than in the city. But at the same time, he wanted to show how sad you can feel in such a landscape – and how lonely. Vincent tried not to worry, but he became sad again. 'I'd really like to write to you about many things, but I sense the pointlessness of it,' he wrote to Theo in the very last letter. He wanted to stay calm. Vincent painted *Tree Roots* on 27 July 1890. But he never finished it. That same day, for the last time, he walked through the fields of Auvers, where he shot himself in the chest with a pistol.

The end

Vincent did not die instantly. Seriously wounded, he walked back to the Auberge Ravoux. Dr Gachet came to see him at once. He wanted to send a message to Theo that same evening. But Vincent wouldn't give him Theo's address. Theo didn't hear about what had happened until the following day. He caught the train to Auvers right away. Vincent lay in his room at the inn, smoking a pipe. He was glad to see his brother, who lay down beside him. For a moment, everything was as it had once been in Zundert: two brothers in one bed. 'Don't worry too much,' Theo wrote to Jo. Vincent had always been strong, so maybe he would recover. But Vincent's injuries were very serious. He died on the morning of 29 July 1890, with Theo by his side.

A sunny place in the wheatfields

Vincent was buried the next day. Friends from Paris came to Auvers to say goodbye. Vincent's coffin was covered with a simple white cloth. His painting equipment was beside it. There were yellow flowers, and the room was full of Vincent's paintings. Dr Gachet brought a huge bouquet of sunflowers because Vincent loved them so much. Someone later wrote that Theo sobbed throughout the funeral. At three in the afternoon, Vincent was taken to the cemetery. 'He is lying in a sunny spot in the middle of the wheatfields,' Theo wrote to Jo the next day. 'I miss him so much. It is as if everything reminds me of him.'

N° 32. — 70e ANNÉE — JEUDI 7 AOUT 1890

L'ÉCHO PONTOISIEN

Journal de l'arrondissement de Pontoise

PARAISSANT LE JEUDI

Un an . . . 8 fr. » Six mois . . . 4 fr. 50

Un an . . . 9 fr. » Six mois . . . 5 fr. »

AGRICULTURE — INDUSTRIE — COMMERCE — LITTÉRATURE — NOUVELLES LOCALES ET FAITS DIVERS

Annonces judiciaires, commerciales et industrielles

— AUVERS-SUR-OISE. — Dimanche 27 juillet, un nommé Van Gogh, âgé de 37 ans, sujet hollandais, artiste peintre, de passage à Auvers, s'est tiré un coup de revolver dans les champs et, n'étant que blessé, il est rentré à sa chambre où il est mort le surlendemain.

A report about Vincent's death in a French newspaper.

AFTER VINCENT'S DEATH

'I can do nothing about it if my paintings don't sell. The day will come, though, when people will see that they're worth more than the cost of the paint,' Vincent once wrote about his paintings. And he was proved right. Shortly before his death, he received many compliments from art experts and artists. Unfortunately, though, Vincent no longer believed in himself. He didn't live to see his paintings become famous all over the world. And sadly, neither did Theo.

What happened to Theo?

After Vincent's death, Theo organized an exhibition of Vincent's paintings in Paris. Not one bit of wall was bare. The people who came to see the exhibition thought the presentation was unusual and beautiful.

But it was a difficult time for Theo. He did indeed resign from the gallery. But he didn't start his own business. That was because he became ill. So ill, in fact, that he could no longer look after himself and his family. His wife Jo took him to the Netherlands. Theo was admitted to a special hospital, but he didn't recover. Six months after Vincent's death, Theo passed away, too.

To the Netherlands

Theo was buried in Utrecht. **Jo** and the young Vincent Willem stayed in the Netherlands. They inherited Vincent's hundreds of drawings and paintings. They hung the art on their walls, and what didn't fit on the walls was stored in the attic. From then on, Jo took care of the collection. She worked hard to support herself and her young son. To make Vincent's work better known, she occasionally sold a piece to a collector or a museum, like *The Starry Night*, for example, which is now famous all over the world.

In 1905, Jo organized a large exhibition at the Stedelijk Museum in Amsterdam, with 472 drawings and paintings by Vincent on display. However, not everyone understood at the time what Vincent's art was about. Someone wrote in the newspaper that the exhibition was 'extremely curious'. Even though it happened slowly, Vincent and his art were becoming more and more famous, thanks to Jo.

Letters

Soon after Vincent's death, Theo wanted to make a book of the letters that Vincent had written. Theo had kept them all, for almost eighteen years. Sadly, he was unable to carry out that plan himself, so Jo took over. It was not an easy task. A large cabinet, filled with letters, had travelled with her from Paris. There were hundreds of them, and they were all jumbled up. First, Jo had to put them in the right order. That was tricky because Vincent often didn't write the date on his letters. Then Jo copied the letters and typed them out. In 1914, her book was finally ready. It was called

Vincent van Gogh. Brieven aan zijn broeder *(Vincent van Gogh – Letters to His Brother)*. That same year, Jo had her husband Theo reburied – not in the Netherlands, but in Auvers-sur-Oise in France. Next to Vincent. She thought the brothers belonged together.

Vincent and the Veluwe

In 1883, Vincent had travelled to the Dutch province of Drenthe. From the train, he had seen the magnificent colours in the Veluwe region. Of course, he had no way of knowing that there would be a museum there fifty years later. And that his own work would be on display in the museum. The Kröller-Müller Museum in Otterlo has 91 paintings and 180 works on paper by Vincent. They were purchased between 1908 and 1929 by **Helene** and Anton Kröller-Müller. It's the second-largest Van Gogh collection in the world. Vincent was Helene's favourite artist, as could be seen after her death. Helene's coffin was displayed in the museum before the funeral, surrounded by her Van Goghs.

The Veluwe is an area of woods and heathland in the middle of the Netherlands.

Vincent's nephew

Twenty-five years after his death, Vincent's work had become very well known. Collectors paid large sums of money for it. People actually made fake 'Van Goghs' because, even back then, there was so much money to be made from selling works by Vincent. When Jo died, the Van Gogh collection went to the young **Vincent Willem**. He was no longer that young, of course. He was older than his father had been when he died, in fact. In 1930, Vincent Willem lent some of his uncle's paintings to the Stedelijk Museum in Amsterdam. He kept others at home in a storage room, and many of them hung on the walls, of course – **just as they once had in his mother's house**.

Amsterdam

More and more people thought that Vincent deserved his own museum. Vincent Willem wanted his uncle's collection to remain together. And one thing led to another. The construction of the **Van Gogh Museum** began in 1969, in Amsterdam. It was designed by a famous Dutch architect, Gerrit Rietveld. By 1973, the museum was finished. Another building was added later, for temporary exhibitions. Millions of people have already visited the museum, and there are more visitors every year.

Vincent worldwide

Vincent's prediction came true. His paintings are worth more now than it cost to make them. Lots more! Vincent's paintings and drawings can be found in museums in every corner of the globe, except for Antarctica. His own journey was far too short; he was only thirty-seven when he died. Vincent went from Z to A: from Zundert in the Netherlands to Auvers-sur-Oise in France. But his story has travelled with his drawings and paintings, all over the world. And that journey is far from over.

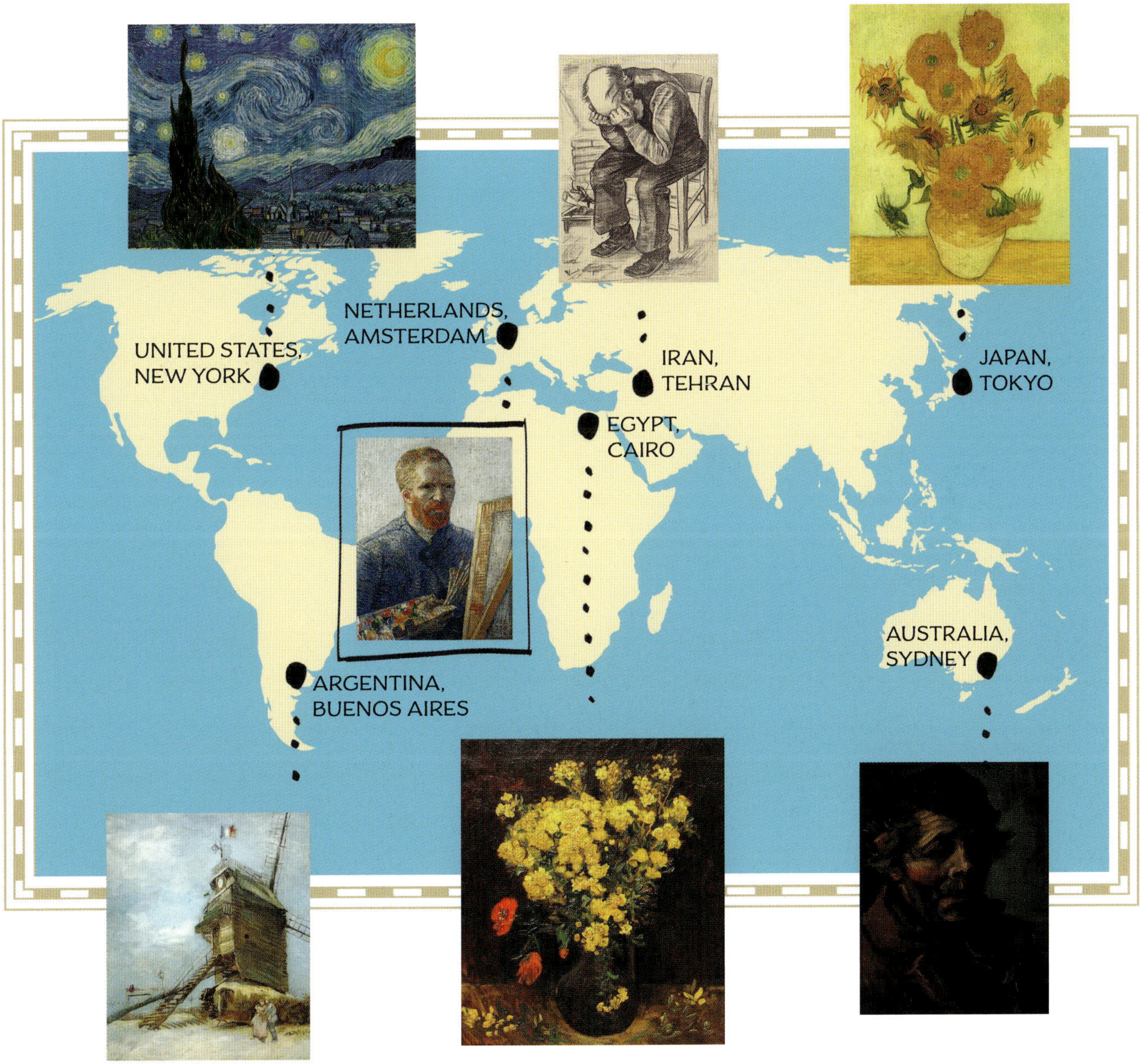

VAN GOGH EUROPE

Nowadays, you can see Vincent's work in museums all over the world. But did you know that you can also visit the places where he lived and worked? More than twenty museums and other places in the Netherlands, Belgium, England and France work together to protect Vincent's legacy. This collaboration is called Van Gogh Europe. Together, these organizations ensure that Vincent's life and work will remain known to people today and also to future generations.
www.routevangogheurope.eu

IMAGE CREDITS

Archives départementales de la Seine-Maritime: p. 24 (top right) | Armand Hammer Museum of Art, Los Angeles: p. 77 | Art Gallery of New South Wales, Sydney: p. 151 (bottom right) | Bijzonder Collecties UvA: pp. 154-155 | Bijzondere Collecties UvA (archive Putman): pp. 42-43 | Bildarchiv Preussischer Kulturbesitz, Berlin: pp. 26-27 | Collection Filip Depuydt: p. 48 (bottom) | Collection Nienke Denekamp: pp. 24 (bottom left), 89 (top), 41 (bottom right), 54-55 (bottom), 84 (bottom), 90 (bottom left), 108 | Collection Oskar Reinhart 'Am Römerholz', Winterthur: pp. 124, 125 (bottom right) | Collection René van Blerk: pp. 48 (top), 84 (top), 127 (top), 138 (bottom left), 140 (top right), 145 (top) | Collection Willem Boorsma: p. 13 (top) | Detroit Institute of Arts, Detroit: p. 98 (row 4, no. 2) | Drents Archief (photo Geert Jannes Landweer): pp. 68-69, 73 | Drents Museum, Assen (photo JAV Studio's): p. 70 (top) | Getty Images, London Stereoscopic Company: p. 25 | Haags Gemeentearchief: pp. 15 (bottom left), 16-17, 60-61, 62 (top, photo C.P. Wollrabe) | J. Paul Getty Museum, Los Angeles: p. 132 (bottom) | Kröller-Müller Museum, Otterlo (photos Rik Klein Gotink): pp. 51 (top), 53 (bottom), 59 (top), 62 (bottom), 64 (middle), 66 (top), 91 (middle), 98 (row 2, no. 3), 112 (top), 115 (top left), 117 (top left), 118 (top right and bottom right), 119 (top left), 131 (top), 149 (bottom) | Kröller-Müller Museum, Otterlo (photo archive): p. 149 (bottom) | Kunsthaus Zürich (gift of Walter Haefner, 1995): p. 114 (bottom right) | Kunstmuseum Basel (on loan from Emily Dreyfus Foundation): p. 98 (row 4, no. 5) | Kunstmuseum Bern (gift of Prof. Dr. Hans R. Hahnloser, Bern): p. 104 (bottom) | Kunstmuseum Den Haag (gift of Fl. Bremmer): p. 65 (bottom) | Kunstmuseum Den Haag: p. 98 (row 1, no. 4) | Library of Congress, Washington: p. 34 (top) | Mohamed Mahmoud Khalil Museum, Cairo: p. 151 (bottom middle) | MoMA, New York: p. 151 (top left) | Municipal Archives Arles: p. 125 (top left) | Musée Angladon, Avignon endpaper front | Musée d'Orsay, Paris (photo tube and palette Erik and Petra Hesmerg): p. 76 | Musée d'Orsay, Paris / RMN-Grand Palais / Adrien Didierjean: pp. 98 (row 5, no. 1), 118 (top left) | Musée d'Orsay, Paris / RMN-Grand Palais / Gérard Blot: p. 142 (top) | Musée d'Orsay, Paris / RMN-Grand Palais / Hervé Lewandowski pp. 109 (bottom right), 140 (top left) | Museo Nacional de Bellas Artes, Buenos Aires: p. 151 (bottom left) | Museum Folkwang, Essen: p. 119 (bottom right) | Museum of Fine Arts, Boston (bequest of John T. Spaulding): p. 138 (bottom right) | Museum of Modern Art, Tehran: p. 151 (top middle) | Neurdein / Roger-Viollet: pp. 92-93 | Paul Sescau: p. 95 (portrait photo Henri de Toulouse-Lautrec) | Petit Palais, Musée des Beaux-Arts de la Ville de Paris (photo painting box Erik and Petra Hesmerg): p. 76 | Princeton University Art Museum (Henry and Rose Pearlman Foundation): p. 114 (bottom left) | Private collection: pp. 104 (top), 115 (top right), 123 (left), 141 (bottom left and bottom right), 142 (bottom left) | Regionaal Archief Dordrecht: p. 37 | Regionaal Archief Tilburg: pp. 12, 13 (middle; bottom, photo Schmidlin) | Rijksmuseum, Amsterdam (photo X. phot): p. 32 | Rijksmuseum, Amsterdam (bequest of Mr and Mrs Drucker-Fraser, Montreux): p. 64 (top) | Rijksmuseum, Amsterdam (gift of F.W.M. Baroness Bonger-van der Borch van Verwolde, Almen): p. 98 (row 2, no. 1) | Seji Togo Memorial Sompo Japan Museum of Art, Tokyo: p. 151 (top right) | Stadsarchief Amsterdam: pp. 40 (Johan Conrad Greive Jr.), 43 (bottom), 44 (middle), 113 (bottom, photo Jacob Olie) | Emil Bührle Collection, on long term loan at Kunsthaus Zürich: pp. 98 (row 5, no. 2), 101 (bottom) | Tate, London: p. 140 (bottom) | The Bancroft Library, University of California, Berkeley: p. 123 (top right) | The Cleveland Museum of Art (bequest of Leonard C. Hanna, Jr.): p. 126 (left) | The Metropolitan Museum of Art, New York: p. 98 (row 5, no. 4) | The Metropolitan Museum of Art, New York (Rogers Fund, 1949): pp. 104 (middle), 142 (bottom left) | The National Gallery, London p. 117: (bottom left) | The Pushkin State Museum of Fine Arts, Moscow: pp. 135 (top), 139 | The State Hermitage Museum, St Petersburg: p. 132 (middle) | Van Gogh Museum, Amsterdam (Archive Tralbaut): pp. 49, 76-77, 123 (bottom right), 125 (bottom left), 131 (bottom), 134 (top right), 142 (top left), 147 | Van Gogh Museum, Amsterdam (State of the Netherlands, bequest of A.E. Ribbius Peletier): p. 135 (bottom) | Van Gogh Museum, Amsterdam (Vincent van Gogh Foundation): pp. 20, 21, 34 (bottom), 52, 53 (top), 57, 64 (bottom left and bottom right), 65 (top), 66 (bottom right), 67 (bottom left), 79, 80, 81, 85, 86 (top), 87, 90 (top), 94, 95 (bottom right), 98 (row 1, nos. 1, 2, 3 and 5; row 2, nos. 2, 4 and 5; row 3, nos. 2, 3, 4 and 5; row 4, nos. 1, 3 and 4; row 5, nos. 3 and 5), 99, 102, 103, 109 (top), 110 (top), 111, 112 (bottom), 113 (top), 114 (top right), 115 (bottom), 116 (top), 117 (top right), 118 (bottom left), 119 (top right, bottom left and bottom middle), 120 (bottom), 121 (bottom left), 130 (bottom), 133, 134 (bottom), 138 (top), 143, 144, 145 (bottom), 146, 151 (middle) | Van Gogh Museum, Amsterdam (Vincent van Gogh Foundation, gift of Paul Gachet Jr.): p. 132 (top) | Veenkoloniaal Museum, Veendam: p. 70 (bottom) | Vincent van GoghHuis, Zundert: p. 11 (top) | Wadsworth Atheneum, Hartford: p. 98 (row 3, no. 1) | West-Brabants Archief: p. 10

The works, drawings, letters and documents that come from the collection of the Van Gogh Museum are the property of the Vincent van Gogh Foundation and are on permanent loan at the museum, with the exception of p. 135 (bottom).

Second edition, 2023

This edition is an adaptation of
The Vincent van Gogh Atlas (2015)

Text: Nienke Denekamp and René van Blerk
Concept *Atlas*: Dik Broekman
With thanks to Teio Meedendorp
Illustrations: Geert Gratama
Design: Yolanda Huntelaar

Publisher: Mascha de Vries (Rubinstein)
Head of Publications: Suzanne Bogman (Van Gogh Museum)
Translation: Laura Watkinson
Coordination: Irene Kunst, Roxanne van den Bosch
Copy-editing: Kate Bell
Image editing: Nienke Denekamp, René van Blerk,
Roxanne van den Bosch

ISBN 9789047630135 | NUR 217
www.rubinstein.nl
www.vangoghmuseum.com

552
fait ~~osé~~ osé espérer
de 80 francs
me chagrine
plus je m'aperçois
que la peinture est un métier qui probablement
est exercé par des gens excessivement pauvres
puisqu'il coûte beaucoup d'argent
Mais l'automne continue encore à être d'un
beau ! quel drôle de pays que cette patrie
de Tartarin. Oui je suis content de mon
sort, c'est pas un pays superbe et sublime
ce n'est que du Daumier bien vivant.
As tu déjà relu les Tartarin ah ne
l'oublie pas ! Te rappelles tu dans Tartarin
la complainte d'~~vieill. omnibus~~
diligence de Tarascon – cette admirable
page – Eh bien je viens de la peindre
cette voiture rouge et verte dans la
cour de l'auberge – Tu verras.
POSTES
15
10 CENTIMES
RAILWAYS OVER WHICH "DISTRICT" COMPANY'S TRAINS RUN